# The Lost History of *Piers Plowman*

THE MIDDLE AGES SERIES

Ruth Mazo Karras, Series Editor
Edward Peters, Founding Editor

A complete list of books in the series is available from the publisher.

# The Lost History of *Piers Plowman*

The Earliest Transmission of Langland's Work

Lawrence Warner

**PENN**

UNIVERSITY OF PENNSYLVANIA PRESS

PHILADELPHIA · OXFORD

Published by
University of Pennsylvania Press
Philadelphia, Pennsylvania 19104–4112

Printed in the United States of America on acid-free paper
10 9 8 7 6 5 4 3 2 1

Library of Congress Cataloging-in-Publication Data
Warner, Lawrence, 1968–
    The lost history of Piers Plowman / Lawrence Warner.
        p.   cm. — (The Middle ages series)
    Includes bibliographical references and index.
    ISBN 978-0-8122-4275-1 (hardcover; alk. paper)
    1. Langland, William, 1330?–1400? Piers Plowman—
Criticism, Textual. 2. Langland, William, 1330?–1400?—
Manuscripts. I. Title.
PR2016.W37   2010
821'.1—dc22                                          2010005650

*For Genevieve, with all my love*

# Contents

*Preface*

Any history of Langland studies must for the most part tell the history of its textual controversies. Is *Piers Plowman* the work of one, or of five? How much emendation of the B archetype is justifiable? Is the Z text authorial, or scribal? Has the power of the alphabet blinded us to the true order in which the versions of the poem were composed? What is the value of John But's testimony, in A 12, to William Langland's poetic career? Middle English scholars are intimately familiar with such questions, because they are so important in defining, not to mention interpreting, *Piers Plowman*. But a problem I take to be more important than any of these has barely registered in critical consciousness. It is deceptively simple: what is the date of the archetypal B manuscript? On its face the question might seem unduly technical and particular. Surely the real issue is when Langland had completed the B version—that, at least, is what critics have focused on in attempting to determine the relation between *Piers Plowman* and, say, the Rising of 1381, or the ideas of John Wyclif. Most if not all offer 1377–78 as the date of that event.[1] Yet the entire surviving record of the B version descends from Bx (as I call this document, following A. V. C. Schmidt), so its dating is the crucial one. If the two individuals we will call the RF and W-M scribes, so called for the manuscripts they in turn generated (R and F in the former case; WHmCrGYOC²CBLM in the latter),[2] did not use Bx as an exemplar till, say, 1393, then the history of *Piers Plowman* needs to be rewritten, beginning to end. It would be difficult to maintain, for instance, that the C version was prompted by the public's reception of B, or that John Ball or Geoffrey Chaucer knew the B version by 1381, to take two major cases.

There are good reasons to pursue this possibility. One of those reasons inheres in the elegant program of textual affiliations, over the course of entire passages of up to forty lines long, between a C-character manuscript and the W-M group where the RF group has nothing or is spurious. Much of this book will present and analyze that and related programs, arguing that they are the result of contamination of Bx by the C text as now attested only in Aberystwyth, National Library of Wales MS 733B, a witness to the earliest stage of *Piers Plowman* C (sigil $N^2$). No one has noticed this because the evidence, which can be presented in relatively simple charts, is dispersed over hundreds of lemmata spread over the three Athlone editions and thus published over a span of some thirty-eight years. Previous assumptions that nothing like this could have occurred had the effect of burying the evidence that undermines those very assumptions. But we do not need to go through all that material to assess the plausibility of the idea that Bx was contaminated by C—indeed, to see that it is likely, perhaps even as certain as the evidence will permit. This instance, while not nearly as complicated as the indications upon which this book focuses, has likewise flown entirely below critics' radar, the reasons for which are as important as the indications themselves. The next few paragraphs will thus not only establish some important groundwork for my argument as a whole, but also serve as a miniature copy of that argument and of the phenomena that have rendered it so contrarian.

Both the local and large-scale cases reveal themselves upon examination of small items that just do not fit the usual narratives of *Piers Plowman*'s production. We need to put on our Sherlock Holmes hats to figure them out. The clues to the local mystery did not become apparent until J. A. Burrow's 2007 essay on the rubrics of the B-version manuscripts, in which, somewhat hidden beneath all the data presented there, we find this little gem: "MS R lacks the whole of Passus XIX and the beginning of XX, but at the end of XX R has 'Passus ii[us] de do best'. Remarkably, L has the same heading (but in its guide only) also at the end of the poem, suggesting perhaps expectation of a further, twenty-first passus. Agreement between L and R here may imply that this anomalous heading was present in the B archetype."[3] Burrow is pulling together various strands of discussion from the previous two decades-plus: MS R's rubric came to light in an essay published in 1985 by Robert Adams;[4] L's in David Benson and Lynne Blanchfield's 1997 catalogue of the B manuscripts;[5] and the import of LR agreements (though of course voiced in ignorance of this instance) in another Adams study, of 2000: "When L agrees with R, even in the face of massive dissenting evidence from the other witnesses, the odds are always quite good that what R and L are mirroring is Bx (albeit the readings of that prototypical copy can never be simply equated with authorial text)."[6]

But Burrow omits to mention a crucial piece of information that would have answered the question of how this bizarre rubric got into Bx in the first place: "Almost certainly it was laterally imported, perhaps into an ancestor of R," wrote Adams, "from a C manuscript (where an identical rubric occurs in the XU family at the beginning of the final passus and a very similar one at the end of the same passus in the majority of all C manuscripts)."[7] In light of his later work and the newly apparent presence of MS L in the picture, we need now to substitute "into Bx" for Adams's "perhaps into an ancestor of R." The B archetype, in sum, was contaminated by the C tradition. Any other explanation for LR's agreement in this error would have an extraordinarily difficult row to hoe.

This conclusion incidentally undermines the argument in whose service Burrow had mentioned it, for if the earliest possible stage of the B-tradition rubrics took shape under the influence of the C tradition, and was erroneous at that, it becomes quite difficult to argue for their authorial nature except on purely literary grounds (and in fact only Burrow and, more recently, Hanna have attempted to do so).[8] Its implications, though, extend far beyond such arcane topics as the authority of the rubrics. For one, the only evidence for the B tradition's existence before the later 1380s or early '90s inheres in the indications of the existence of at most two copies, the C reviser's B manuscript and possibly the document to which a scribe in MS F's line of transmission had access.[9] And it also means that Bx was the product of an era in which readers of *Piers Plowman* began to become "jealous for the completeness of their copies," in George Kane's words.[10] This should immediately prompt us to wonder, for instance, whether this mistaken rubric was the only item that came into B from the C tradition: might, say, the entire final two passus have been part of this contamination? And to what extent should we assent to the editorial assumption that this could not have occurred?

*The Lost History of "Piers Plowman"* follows up on these questions, answering with a resounding "yes" and "not at all" respectively. It has two major aims: to lay out the evidence leading to this conclusion, which is far more extensive than what is found in LR's final rubric, and to show that the previous silence about that possibility is not an index to its plausibility, but, rather, the product of the assumption that B was integral. That the only information regarding the LR situation offered by the Kane-Donaldson and Schmidt editions is that MS R has a distinctive rubric on its final folio—nothing about what the rubric says, or L's role—shows that we need to go beyond their analyses and methodologies as we assess the earliest production and transmission of the poem.[11] Chapter 1 examines in some detail the claims made in the service of the beliefs that B was widely available by c. 1380 and its converse, that *Piers Plowman* A did *not* achieve substantial circulation until well after its own composition, perhaps even until some decades into the fifteenth century. Some of these popular claims rely on a few codicological indicators, and others, on assumptions concerning supposed allusions to B around 1380. The chapter mines a body of evidence all but neglected in such discussions, that of the textual affiliations, which leads to the opposite conclusion: the A version was widely available, while its immediate successor, B, might not even have gone beyond the poet's immediate circle till the 1390s or so.

Chapter 2 opens by querying the assumptions, first, that each of the three major textual traditions of the poem was at its origin integral and unaffected by the others, and second, that any indications that suggest otherwise are the result of convergent variation, the means by which unrelated manuscripts attest unauthorial variants not sourced from a mutually exclusive ancestor. Only slightly less powerful is the conviction that conflation—which is what I will argue was a major force in the production of our received B version— always manifests itself in scribal officiousness, such as inconsequence, bad sense, or repetition. None of these is well founded, as the pattern of affiliations summarized above reveals. This chapter examines the means by which MS $N^2$'s "B" readings have been exiled from the B edition—or, to be more accurate, how W-M's "C" ones have been kept from the C edition.

The primary mode of this "contamination," Chapter 3 shows, was via the movement of passages on sheets of loose revision material that could go easily from Langland's C papers to Bx as copied by the W-M subarchetypal scribe. The converse notion, that such loose papers went in the opposite direction, stumbles for a number of reasons, not least the fact that there is no evidence (unless this pattern is the sole exception) that the B continuation comprised such materials while the C additions, as E. Talbot Donaldson said, "were probably written on separate sheets and their position in the text indicated by one of those complicated systems of arrows and carets that every reviser finds himself adopting."[12] This chapter demonstrates the point via a focus upon the fortunes of a passage whose textual state serves as a litmus test for any belief in such an integral "B version": the forty lines in which Langland inveighs against "the poison of possession" and calls for clerical disendowment (received B 15.533–69). (All references to passus, line numbers, and sigils are to the Athlone editions, whose conventions I apply silently to those quotations and references to other schemes—e.g., different line numbers in Schmidt or passus numbers in Skeat's; see further below on my policies. I do not reproduce editorial brackets.[13]) It is already well known that these lines are misplaced in W-M and absent from RF. What no one has known before is that $N^2$ attests them in precisely the "B" form, and the only viable solution to this mess is ur-C > Bx contamination.

Chapter 4 argues, primarily on the basis of textual affiliations—this time not so much $N^2$/W-M as that pattern's converse, RF/C—that the final two passus were among the C-tradition materials that intruded into B. Again, the assumption that the archetypal texts, Bx and Cx, could be established without regard to the evidence of the other tradition has hampered recognition that, whatever the reason, something very odd is going on in these passus. There is no way that accident could explain the extent to which RF and C agree in this portion of the poem alone. To date, though, no one has been able even to suggest a solution to the problem because our ways of thinking about *Piers Plowman* have prevented recognition of the problem in the first place. If my own solution—that these passus were not in any "B-version" manuscripts that might have circulated prior to the appearance of C—is viable, then some of the central objects of Middle English studies, ranging from the character of the C revision to the beginnings of "lollardy," look much different from what we have assumed.

The patterns of affiliations that give rise to this argument confirm the interpretation of the LR "passus ii$^{us}$ de Dobest" rubric given above, which already would be very difficult to explain otherwise. Yet this idea that Bx was contaminated by the C tradition, while it might seem surprising or even iconoclastic, has in fact already made its mark upon the received B version. For the Athlone editors themselves assumed Bx's contamination by C, though they buried their statement to that effect in a subordinate clause, in support of a very minor emendation of the C archetype, discussed on the 557th of their 572 pages of prose.[14] Schmidt judges their discussion "incomprehensible,"[15] and indeed they do not see the need to present any evidence of the claim beyond their judgment that a single line in Bx came from C. If, though, they had been explicit about this belief in their earlier, long analysis of the character of the B archetype, and had drawn out the clear implications, Langland studies' embrace of the assumption of B's early and wide readership might not have been quite as fervent as it has turned out to be.

Nor, perhaps, would the authority with which critics have invested the surviving manuscripts have had such a firm hold on the field. Much of the controversy surrounding the Athlone edition was in effect a manifestation of this desire to collapse the work (i.e., what we mean by *"Piers Plowman* B") into the text of a given document (e.g., the words as presented in Trinity

College Cambridge MS B.15.17, MS W, copy-text for the Kane-Donaldson and Schmidt editions). Langland studies are not alone in struggling with the effects and difficulties of this desire. Paul Eggert's book *Securing the Past* is helpful to those negotiating this dilemma via its proffering of a new definition of "the work" as an entity "constantly involved in a negative dialectic of material medium (the documentary dimension) and meaningful experience (the textual), and as being constituted by an unrolling semiosis across time, necessarily interwoven in the lives of all who create it, gaze at it or read it."[16]

An earlier generation of editors assumed that "the work" existed quite apart from their own interventions, prompting some recent commentators to react by dispensing altogether with the editorial enterprise, preferring to celebrate, rather than analyze, scribal variants, or to urge a return to manuscripts and the abandonment of author-driven textual reconstruction. I am all for greater emphasis on manuscripts in the study of *Piers Plowman*, but do not see the need to reject editions as part of that project. Complicit in certain idealist fantasies Middle English textual editing may be; but, as Lee Patterson says, "if the humanist premises that have underwritten textual criticism in the past are now to be dismissed, what is to take their place?" As he points out, "the refusal to edit—which is part of the larger refusal to interpret—is an all too tenacious tradition within medieval studies."[17]

This impasse between pure idealism and pure Aristotelianism, as it were, needs breaking if we are not simply to recycle earlier critical paradigms by default. As Eggert concludes, "securing tangible and intangible works from the past, whether historic buildings, paintings or literary works, means facing up to (and often differentiating) their intertwined documentary and textual dimensions." He stresses "agency and chronology, especially as they inflect and determine the production-consumption spectrum," as the closely related themes that emerge at points of crisis in the work of conservation. "Together they point towards the need for a broader understanding of the *work* than the 1960s bequeathed us."[18] Eggert's approach, while it takes the Gabler-Kidd debate over *Ulysses* and the concept of the "materialist Shakespeare" as its primary literary instances, provides a robust framework for future thinking about the *Piers Plowman* situation. Indeed, in many ways it applies to *Piers Plowman* more than to almost any other "work," given the importance of chronology and nonauthorial agents in the production of the various versions. The basic goal of this book, then, is to face up to the intertwined documentary and textual dimensions of the work we call *Piers Plowman* by identifying, as precisely as possible given our historical distance, the modes of its production at given times and places. The subject of the "lost history" I am narrating is not just the newly identified, "ur-B" version of the poem, but also the well-known stages of text whose histories have been lost as well. The received "B version," which I identify as owing its shape as much to scribal or readerly desires for "complete" texts as to its author's aesthetic vision, is no less authentic a part of the "work" *Piers Plowman* than is the earlier, previously unknown one, but its character, and its place on the production-consumption spectrum, have remained obscure.

Langland studies' wholesale embrace of Adam Pinkhurst rather than William Langland as the figure in whose language we quote its most canonical version already elevates the status of scribal responses to the poem. There is no problem with that policy in itself: Pinkhurst's work on Trinity B.15.17 is just as much part of the work *Piers Plowman* as is any other text.[19] But a sharpening of our awareness of what it means to quote "the B version," that is, Langland's poem (as most critics continue to say they are doing), in his language will only bolster our understanding of that work's production and consumption. Kane-Donaldson and Schmidt chose MS W as copy-text, the text that determines spelling only and never choice of lection, because Pinkhurst was consistent in his language, made it more inviting to modern readers reared on the Chaucer manuscripts he also copied, and was fortunate that no other surviving B copies surpassed his in those regards.[20] It also bolstered Pinkhurst's impact that Kane and Donaldson were working "in default of any evidence about the original dialect of the poem," believing that "there is no evidence that [Langland] wrote *Piers Plowman* in that native dialect, any more than that he retained this in adulthood."[21]

But our knowledge of dialects has increased substantially since 1975. M. L. Samuels has shown that the reconstruction of Langland's dialect, *at all stages of his career*, "could probably be best achieved by adopting X [of C; San Marino, Huntington Library MS Hm 143] as the basis and modifying it in a conservative direction."[22] This was the language "that he used in his holographs," including those of the A and B traditions.[23] Remnants of this fact sometimes appear in places where the copy-text overextends its reach and forces editors to treat its readings as substantives in need of emendation, as at W's B 20.198, "So Elde and she hadden it forbeten," which appears in Kane and Donaldson as "So Elde and [heo] hadden it forbeten," so as to restore alliteration by adopting the C tradition's dialectal form of the term *she*. R. W. Chambers observed about the *Piers Plowman* manuscripts in 1935, well before Greg's famous rationale said the same thing, that "we are dependent,

in the matter of dialect and spelling, to a much greater degree than we are in
the matter of wording, upon our basic manuscript, and it is therefore all the
more vital to select a well spelled manuscript, containing no spelling which
we have reason to think the original writer would not have used."[24] If he was
right—and the entire premise of copy-text theory that the Athlone editors
follow suggests he was—then we ought now, if seeking to print the poem in
Langland's language (by no means the only option, but the one I am adopt-
ing in this book), to stop doing so in Pinkhurst's and begin doing so in that
of MS X.

Some critics have thus criticized Kane and Donaldson's choice of Trinity
as copy-text,[25] but that seems both unfair, given when they were working,
and beside the more important point that we are not bound to adopt their
approach in our own quotations of the poem. Thus, when I am not quoting
directly from a manuscript, I quote from C as presented in Russell and Kane's
edition, which uses X as its copy-text, because that suits my own purpose
of representing Langland's poetry in a language closer to his own than any
otherwise available. And to remain true to that purpose, and consistent in my
practice, I translate the language of the published editions of the A and B ver-
sions (i.e., of MSS T and W) into the language of MS X as well. If the transla-
tion of the language of received A and B into that of C strikes any readers as
too intrusive, they should remember that the Athlone editions are full of such
"translated" passages—B 20.198 as cited above is one instance in which they
do exactly on a local level what I will do throughout. Indeed one of the main
purposes of a copy-text is precisely to guide editors on the presentation of
lines and passages absent from that text; among the 170-odd lines not in MS
W that Kane and Donaldson translate into that text's language are B 15.511–
28, which will play an important role in this book. Before the appearance of
Joseph Wittig's *Concordance* in 2001 my approach would have been almost
impossible; now, though, it is relatively painless, even rather enjoyable, and
productive of a more intimate knowledge of the cited A and B passages than
simple transcription of the edited texts would have permitted.[26]

It seems quite possible—almost certain, if we are to assume that Kane
would have followed his own convictions to their logical conclusions—that
Kane, alone and with Donaldson, would have adopted this approach had
he had access to Wittig's invaluable work. Twenty years after the B edition,
collaborating with Janet Cowen, he wanted to edit Chaucer's *Legend of Good
Women* in part because doing so "would illustrate the problem of copy text in
the instance of fourteenth-century poetry preserved only in fifteenth-century

or late fifteenth-century manuscripts."[27] The problem was that, whereas "there are manuscripts of both *Troilus and Criseyde* and *The Canterbury Tales* admirably suited to serve as copy text in Greg's sense"—that is, as provider of language, *not* as "base text" that supplies the most correct readings—the same does not apply for Chaucer's other works.[28] His conclusion is bold: he chooses the text in Oxford, Bodleian MS Tanner 346 because "it represents authentically what run-of-the-mill fifteenth-century scribes made of, did to, Chaucer's language. For editors of Chaucer's minor works use of such a manuscript is one alternative. The other is to rewrite the poem in the language presumed to be Chaucer's. This would bring to the fore new issues of rationale."[29]

In suggesting that copy-text is only one of two viable approaches to this problem, Kane here added his voice to a growing consensus. Fredson Bowers himself had suggested something like my policy.[30] Now Joseph Dane has endorsed this approach with regard to the closest post-medieval equivalent to the phenomenon of *Piers Plowman*: "That a copy-text must be a version of the text to be edited seems obvious enough, but there could be situations where this might not be the case, e.g., where a 'version' of a text is regarded not as a 'variant' but as a *different text*. The Folio *King Lear* could easily be edited with the Quarto functioning as copy-text, even by an editor who regards them as representing different plays."[31] And finally G. Thomas Tanselle has urged that in situations of "radiating authority"—again, such as *Piers Plowman*, though he does not here say as much—editors should edit without a copy-text.[32]

So, too, I would suggest, might critics of *Piers Plowman* benefit from citing without an edition. The collapse of text into document has been occurring for too long on the level of editions, as well as copy-texts. To grant Kane and Donaldson's or Schmidt's editions status as "*Piers Plowman* B," the work itself, rather than as one of many ways of representing that entity, is not fair either to that entity or to what they were attempting to achieve. The Athlone editors were working in the absence of knowledge we now have, and upon which we can now act. The decision to print A and B in a language different from that of their respective editions is in keeping with this book's argument that *Piers Plowman* is a much more fluid concept than is represented by separate (or parallel) editions each of which assumes that the archetypal origins of the versions are integral.

As such, I hope that this book will go some way towards recuperating "the work" as a helpful, a necessary, category in those constructions of literary history that attend closely to manuscript cultures. The collapse of work into document might have more dramatic consequences in *Piers Plowman* than it would on, say, Chaucer studies, which probably explains the alacrity with which critics have embraced it in their attempts to downplay or even dismiss the editorial achievements of previous generations. If what survives is a fair representation of what preceded it, why bother to discover any lost past? Indeed. But if, as this book argues, what survives is something else entirely, then we owe it to those extant documents, not to mention to the author or authors, executors, scribes, censors, readers, collectors, editors, and critics to begin again the hard work of reconstituting the work in a form capacious enough to make room for the lost history of *Piers Plowman*.

# Chapter 1

# *Piers Plowman* Before 1400:
# Evidence for the Earliest Circulation
# of A, B, and C

William Langland was finished with *Piers Plowman* A by around 1370, but its earliest extant manuscripts are no earlier than about 1390.[1] Such gaps are not unusual for Middle English poetry,[2] but the existence of *Piers Plowman* in so many versions, and the indications that major figures like John Ball and Geoffrey Chaucer knew one of those versions as early as 1380, render our response to this gap in particular especially urgent. The predominant narrative of the poem's early existence—that the B version was the only one available by that date—is in effect a gloss on that gap, one that assumes that A manuscripts from the 1370s do not survive now because they did not exist in the first place. But that narrative passes in silence over the fact that no B manuscripts survive from that era either. At least for the sake of consistency, one might hope for the acknowledgment that the dates of extant manuscripts indicate nothing about the form in which *Piers Plowman* existed by 1380.

For a much fuller mapping of the earliest circulation of *Piers Plowman* we need to turn to another major and widely available, if also widely neglected, area of knowledge: the status of the texts within these manuscripts. This material, I will argue, directs us to the conclusion that, contrary to widespread belief, *Piers Plowman* A achieved a substantial circulation from very early stages, the B version in contrast remaining dormant until readers and scribes had embraced the final, C version. I then turn to the external indications that have a bearing on the question of the B version's early availability, found in works written by a pamphleteer, a poet, and a preacher c. 1381–82; again, I will show that A is the most likely source of their knowledge. This chapter sets in train the central theme of this book: the earliest production and transmission of *Piers Plowman* were nothing like what we have assumed.

## Evidence for the Early Circulation of *Piers Plowman* A

The gap between the composition of *Piers Plowman* A and its surviving manuscripts invites two competing interpretations. One is best articulated by Ian Doyle, who finds it "not surprising that the earliest copies of Langland's A text, composed in the 1360s and perhaps slow to be multiplied, but increasingly sought after, should have been lost, as the other longer texts became available for preference, combination or conflation."[3] This approach has the advantages of speaking to the character of A in particular, as such forces of destruction would not apply to B or C, and of being immune to disproval. Only the sudden revelation of dozens of ancient A-version manuscripts would alter the point, and even then it would still seem likely that innumerable others were victims to the desire for longer versions. Still, Ralph Hanna, in voicing the alternative approach, goes so far as to censure Doyle's as one that "simply ignores the visible historical evidence," which instead, he writes, "suggests that this version had absolutely minimal circulation before about 1425."[4]

Hanna immediately qualifies this remark, though, acknowledging that three A-version manuscripts are "certainly fourteenth-century": Cambridge, Trinity College, MS R.3.14 (T; 1 in our running count of pre-1400 manuscripts); the "Vernon" text, in Oxford, Bodleian MS Eng. Poet. a.1 (V; 2); and the infamous MS Z (Oxford, Bodleian MS Bodley 851; 3).[5] The "evidence for other pre-1400 copies" prompts a further retreat:[6] the exemplar or ancestor shared by Bodleian Library, MS Rawlinson poet. 137 (R) and Oxford, University College MS 45 (U), whose reference to Richard II as monarch in its passus 12 indicates its pre-1399 date (4; Schmidt's u);[7] the copy available to Scribe D as he wrote the Ilchester manuscript (J of C), whose Prologue incorporates material from A and a variant C tradition (5);[8] and that used by the scribe of the common archetype behind the BmBoCot group (6).

Hanna's list of now-lost A manuscripts is very selective. Many more than these three are necessary to explain the surviving affiliations, as the accounts of George Kane and A. V. C. Schmidt in their respective editions make clear. It is true enough that manuscripts cannot be dated very precisely, "erroneous readings" are the products of subjective reasoning, the results are inevitably incomplete, and stemmata are of limited use, at best, to editors. But as

Hanna elsewhere says, "However editors may use stemmata in textual re-construction, the diagrams themselves do represent historical processes, and processes capable of some degree of specification."[9] A little common sense, such as not assuming a direct correlation between the number of lost and extant manuscripts in any given version, will more than balance any potential problems.[10]

For beginners, a quick glance at Schmidt's diagram of the A tradition reveals the existence of nine additional lost copies, all those in the lines of de-scent culminating in MSS T and V.[11] MS T's ancestry includes TH[2] (7); t (8), ancestor of TH[2]Ch; d (9), ancestor of TH[2]ChD; $r^1$ (10), exemplar of d and u; **r** (11), exemplar of $r^1$ and $r^2$ (the latter being the ancestor of VHJLKWNZ); Ax (12), ancestor of all surviving copies; and A-Ø (13), a pre-archetypal copy.[12] And MS V's ancestry comprises v (14)[13] and $r^2$ (15). But even this is a partial tally. Kane says that the corrupted character of V "presuppos[es] a consider-able number of stages of transmission,"[14] a point supported by M. L. Samu-els's remark that some of V's dialect forms suggest that, unlike others in the A tradition, including H, "it was derived from an eastern exemplar,"[15] very unlikely to be v itself, and thus constituting item (16).[16] The affiliations of the text of folios 124–39 of Bodley 851 ("the Z version") with MSS (E)A(W) MH[3], the **m** group, show that **m** or its ancestor must predate that very early manuscript, thus constituting item (17).[17]

And there is no reason to restrict ourselves to the affiliations of the rela-tively complete A-version manuscripts. Item 6, the copy behind the A matter in BmBoCot, bears a close relation to the t-group, especially MS H[2]. These affiliations are most probably explained, as Carl Grindley has shown, by posit-ing an exclusive ancestor (18) of 6 and 7, with MS T's correct readings against H[2]BmBoCot representing scribal improvements to a faulty exemplar's read-ings.[18] And Russell and Kane characterize the Ilchester MS's A frame text, copied from 5, as "ordinary: in about twenty departures from the adopted A text it enters more than a dozen different agreements."[19] But this is misleading, for its mere fifty-two lines share six errors with the mid-fifteenth-century MS W alone, and another three with W and one other witness or group.[20] This is about the densest rate of error in the surviving manuscript record.[21] Unless W descends directly from the very exemplar behind MS J, and unless that exem-plar was a direct copy of Ax, by the 1390s at least one now-lost generator of the family to which MSS W and J belong, number (19), must have been extant.

So wild are the A-text affiliations that nearly every member tends to fol-low the pattern represented so far by MS V. Hanna, contradicting his earlier stern judgment, has pointed out that the "impenetrable dialectal mixtures" of the A manuscripts constitute a state of affairs that "suggests that many manuscripts are the surviving product of several generations of copyings in diverse locales."[22] And while these "generations" are stages of copying in lines of transmission rather than fixed periods of time, it takes time for manuscripts to be copied, travel, and find new scribes and audiences. All of which is to say that the figure of nineteen now-lost A manuscripts is the result of the most efficient explanation of textual affiliations; only once, in the case of MS V, did we even begin to make use of the dialectal data here cited by Hanna. The wildness of the A tradition's textual record alone, not to mention its impenetrable dialectal mixtures, should have put the restraints upon all the rhetoric about its supposedly late circulation.

It remains unclear how long before 1400 or so the A tradition achieved wide circulation. MS T's distance from Ax—some six generations of copying—does not necessitate, even if it might imply, a very lengthy period of time. The earliest surviving manuscripts with A material are probably Vernon and Ilchester, but they might be only three or so generations from the archetype. It is clear, though, that since 1960 plenty of evidence for *Piers Plowman* A's substantial fourteenth-century readership has been available. Readers have on the whole ignored this remarkable body of data, focusing their energies and anxieties instead on the established Athlone text. But it enables a much more thorough mapping of the shady terrain in which *Piers Plowman* first circulated than do the dates of the extant witnesses.

## Lost: *Piers Plowman* B

The corollary to the belief that A had no public life in the fourteenth century is the assumption that B, by contrast, "quickly achieved something like a canonical status," as Robert Adams has put it.[23] Yet the earliest extant B manuscripts, like those of A, date to the 1390s.[24] More problematic is that the B tradition's "tightly bifid stemma" below, which Adams produced on the basis of work done by the editors of the *Piers Plowman Electronic Archive*, is suggestive, as he says, of "a tradition that never consisted of many manuscripts."[25] A total of eight now-lost manuscripts (in bold: Bx, two in the α family, five in β) are necessary to explain the relationships among the survivors; see chart.[26]

All eight lost B-tradition manuscripts, and at most about five extant ones, are likely or possible products of the 1390s. Given the tenor of most discussions

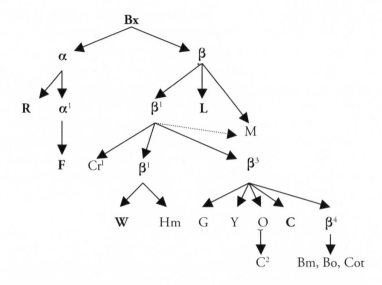

of the early transmission of *Piers Plowman*, the fact that the number of pre-1400 manuscripts necessitated by the A tradition's affiliations is about 50 percent greater than this figure might seem surprising in itself. But most striking here are how well defined the B tradition is (quite opposed to A), and how *late* it came into being. Two of the extant fourteenth-century productions, plus one dated to the beginning of the fifteenth century (B.L. MS Add. 35287 [M]), are only two generations of copying removed from the archetype.

The notion that B achieved something like a canonical status between its postulated date of completion (c. 1377–78) and, say, the Rising of 1381, then, is an assumption rather than a postulate based on textual evidence. Schmidt is the only critic to have explained his belief that Bx was a product of the late 1370s in positive terms, and he carefully presents the case as a matter of probabilities and presumptions: "it is likely to be the longer version that the peasant rebel leaders alluded to in 1381," he claims, on which basis he later says that B's "archetypal manuscript was presumably generated only a couple of years before the Rising [of 1381]."[27] The substance of this proposal, Ball's presumed knowledge of B, will occupy us below; but the fact remains that the only pre-archetypal manuscripts inferable on textual grounds are the C reviser's B manuscript and the copy to which the F or $\alpha^1$ scribe had access, which the Athlone account necessitates. And some critics have cast doubt upon the existence of even these two, particularly with regard to F.[28] Robert Adams has interpreted the "multilayered complexity of dialects" in the B tradition as "indicative of a wider circulation (and more extensive recopying) than that achieved by the C version," but in fact there is no compelling reason to attribute these layers to any more than the three-plus post-archetypal generations represented above.[29] Anyone eager to use this evidence to bolster the count of early B copies, if playing fair, will need to follow suit with regard to the "impenetrable dialectal mixtures" of the A manuscripts.[30]

In sum, if the messy state of affairs in which the A version survives looks exactly like the result of a tradition whose ancestors had disappeared, the cleanness of B's makes it look as though it never had such ancestors.[31] This cleanness, and not the absence of early A copies, presents the most pressing question about the earliest transmission of A and B. Almost fifty years ago in Sydney, George Russell spoke to the heart of the matter: "Why is it," he wondered,

> that that version of the poem which almost all modern readers and critics agree in judging to be the most impressive, was the version whose lines of survival were most tenuous; which, in fact, seems to have escaped extinction only by the chance survival of a single manuscript? It may be that this was a mere matter of accident: but the facts of the A- and C-descent suggest that this is unlikely. If the short and essentially incomplete A-text finds readers and copyists in numbers from the beginning, and if the same is also true of C-, why then should B- not find them?[32]

By way of explanation Russell proposed that B, "for various reasons, mostly political, religious and ideological, was either called in by the author or was suppressed by others," of which destructive program Bx was a chance survivor.[33] But what mechanisms could have enabled so thorough a suppression? If this version was circulating widely, how did Langland or these other censors know how many copies were extant, where to find them, and how to prevent further copying?[34] A more efficient explanation, if one less conducive to most narratives of the history of *Piers Plowman*, is that Langland's own B version achieved absolutely minimal circulation, if any at all, before c. 1395, and not very much between then and 1550 either.

## The Early Proliferation of the C Version

The most likely scenario is that readers' quick embrace of *Piers Plowman* C led to the release of the dormant B version.[35] This claim follows from the fact that

C's transmission history differs so starkly from those of A and B. Far more of its manuscripts predate 1400, and four manuscripts from Schmidt's collective sigil y (XYHJ) have excited particularly strong interest. These texts exhibit both dialectal features very close to those presumed to be Langland's, which many critics have taken as evidence of his whereabouts when he composed C, and codicological and paleographical characteristics very similar to those of the London-based productions associated with Gower and Chaucer.[36] In two of these, San Marino, Huntington Library MS Hm 143 (X) and the Ilchester manuscript (J), critics have found evidence of "some direct connection to the author."[37] Such judgments, however, have not taken account of these surviving manuscripts' positions within the C stemma. Ten surviving witnesses— three of these four (XHJ), plus MSS UTPEVMK—predate 1400, as do some fourteen more now-lost copies in Schmidt's chart.[38] MS X alone, like MS T in the A tradition, is some five to eight generations of copying removed from Langland's holograph.[39] Even if Langland was alive when C entered circulation, the chances of his survival diminish with each successive generation. We should be wary of any placement of MS X or J in close physical or even textual proximity to the author.

This body of data should also prompt a fresh analysis of our methodologies of dating the versions. In recent years, a *terminus a quo* of 1388 for the completion of C has gained widespread support on the basis of Anne Middleton's argument that the *apologia pro vita sua* (C 5.1–104) stages an interrogation under the 1388 Statute of Laborers.[40] The most surprising of this proposal's many adherents is George Kane, who adds that "the latest topicality in C appears to be reference to the king's implacable hatred of Gloucester and the Arundels after the dissolution of the Merciless Parliament (C 5.194–96)," that is, the months following June 1388.[41] If so, we must marvel at the extraordinary rapidity with which early scribes set to work on C. Although this scenario is not impossible, it is much more difficult than has been acknowledged by most accounts of C's early production, which seem to assume that Cx or other early manuscripts were available for copying at will by any given fourteenth-century scribe.

## The Evidence of Allusion?

Kathryn Kerby-Fulton's 2006 study *Books Under Suspicion* represents a major recent trend in claiming to identify allusions to the B version in works

composed by 1382 at the latest. In the lines "With an O and an I, Si tunc ta-
cuisses / Tu nunc stulto similis philosophus fuisses" from the 1382 broadside
"Heu quanta desolacio" (which includes the phrase "rogo dicat Pers"), she
finds a probable reference to B 11.416α, *"Philosophus esses si tacuisses,"* "you
might have been a philosopher, if you had been able to hold your tongue";[42]
later, she describes Chaucer's "Thoo gan y wexen in a were" (*House of Fame*,
979) as a "deliberate echo" of Will's "And in a wer gan y wex" (B 11.116).[43]
Kerby-Fulton finds "the hints of 'Heu's' Langlandianism . . . significant since
its date is so early in the period of B transmission."[44]

Such proposals are "soft," as it were, in occupying no more difficult a
place than would the idea that, say, a given Shakespearean phrase comes from
Chaucer. They can be adjudicated on the terms in which they are presented—
linguistic, thematic—without regard to questions of transmission. The fact
that no evidence supports the notion of B's transmission by this stage, though,
makes for a dilemma. Can we elevate their status to "hard," constituting posi-
tive evidence, rather than derivative support, for B's early circulation? Some
have had no trouble doing so: one critic announces that a study finding B's
influence in John Ball's letters "establishes that June 1381 is a terminus well
*post quem* for the B version";[45] another says that a similar and separate claim
regarding the *House of Fame* "demonstrates that the B text was probably cir-
culating and known about in London at the time when Chaucer was living
in Aldgate."[46] The assumption, in other words, generates the proposal, which
in turn becomes the evidence upon which the assumption was presumably
based in the first place. While those readers predisposed for whatever reason
to believe in B's transmission c. 1380 might well cite such claims as support-
ing indicators, I think it is fair to say that, when analyzed apart from that
assumption, they remain securely in the "soft" category. Each such claim is
either more easily explicable by recourse to other modes of influence (if any at
all) or contradicts other, equally persuasive proposals, tossing us back to the
very category of evidence we were seeking to bypass.

The appearance of the Latin item shared by "Heu" and the B version in
both Odo of Cheriton's thirteenth-century *Fables* (as I have recently discov-
ered) and John Bromyard's mid-fourteenth century, and hugely influential,
*Summa Praedicantium* (as Alford pointed out and Kerby-Fulton acknowl-
edges), for instance, indicates a mutual indebtedness to the homiletic tradi-
tion c. 1380 rather than one's reliance upon the other.[47] Much more promising
is the parallel between the protagonists of *Piers Plowman* B and the *House
of Fame* who "waxed in a were," that is, "grew into a condition of doubt or

anxiety."[48] Yet Paul and Dante, not Langland, are the most obvious models for Geoffrey's situation here,[49] and only slightly less immediate is Boethius, on the dreamer's mind at this point (*HF* 972), who also "leaves us in fact with much the same kind of doubt that Chaucer now confesses to," says J. A. W. Bennett, citing our line.[50] When Chaucer wrote *were*, he was probably aiming for elegance, given that the alternative, from Philosophy's diagnosis of Boethius's affliction, was this: "thilke passiouns that ben waxen hard in swellynge by perturbacions flowyinge into thy thought."[51] Whichever option he chose, he would have almost certainly needed to use the term *wax*, which appears juxtaposed with these phrases not just in the *House of Fame*, the B version, and *Boece*, but also in Chaucer's account of poor Hypermnestra, who "waxes" cold when she "falls" into a *were*:

> As colde as eny froste now wexeth she
> For pite bi the herte streyneth her so
> And drede of deth doth her so moche wo
> That thryes down she fill in suche a were.[52]

Both Langland and Chaucer are making best use of a psychological vocabulary that is already inherently alliterative. There is no need to attribute the parallels of these lines to anything other than this common body of sounds and ideas.

This is somewhat unfair to Kerby-Fulton's proposal, which appeared in a critical milieu that not only took B's earliness and A's belatedness for granted, but also had been deeply influenced by Frank Grady's argument that the *House of Fame* relied on B. Both poems, he says, interrogate authorities and authoritative discourses, use signatures at moments of poetic transition, and are potentially endless.[53] Whatever the strengths of these suggestive parallels—many of which would fit A, too—they run up against Helen Cooper's equally compelling claim that the *General Prologue* to the *Canterbury Tales* (1387 at the earliest) adopts the A version's Prologue as a model.[54] Grady's Chaucer was particularly taken by the unresolved conclusion of B (i.e., passus 20) in the late 1370s, but Cooper's remained ignorant of B passus 19–20 in the 1380s.[55] Any adjudication would need to take recourse to other evidence—showing that Grady does not "demonstrate" B's availability in the 1370s. The force of George Economou's comments is clear: "wherever critical interpretation leads on the fellowship of Chaucer and Langland, it cannot avoid the mediation of ongoing bibliographical bulletins. Its steps into new pastures will always be dogged or herded, so to speak, by concomitant movements concerning the poems'—mainly Langland's—provenance and dispersal."[56]

The case of John Ball is especially pressing. For one, his letters inciting the Rising of 1381 refer directly to "Peres Plouȝman" ("Heu"'s "Pers" is the closest analogue above). More important, it is almost universally accepted that this appropriation of his poem was a primary instigator of the C revisions.[57] Ball's letter to the commons of Essex, as recorded by Thomas Walsingham, is the most fruitful of the Langlandian letters:

> Johon Schep . . . biddeþ Peres Plouȝman go to his werk, and chastise
> wel Hobbe þe Robbere, and taketh wiþ ȝow Johan Trewman, and alle
> hiis felawes, and no mo, and loke schappe ȝou to on heved, and no mo.
>> Johan þe Mullere haþ ygrounde smal, smal, smal;
>> Þe Kynges sone of hevene schal paye for al.
>> Be war or ȝe be wo;
>> Knoweth ȝour freende fro ȝour foo;
>> Haveth ynow, & seith "Hoo";
>> And do wel and bettre, and fleth synne,
>> And sekeþ pees, and hold ȝou þerinne;
> and so biddeth Johan Trewaman and alle his felawes.[58]

Attempts to identify the version known to Ball, whether directly or via oral transmission, falter on the fact that all three of the relevant phrases (four, if one counts "John Sheep" as a reference to A Prol.2/B Prol.2) appear in both A and B: not just *Peres Plouȝman*, but also *Hobbe the Robbere* (A 5.233, B 5.461) and *do wel and bettre* (Dobet: A passus 9–11, B passus 8–14).

Yet most recent commentators simply accept as a given that Ball knew the B rather than the A version.[59] Some of those who cite the lateness of A manuscripts, such as Steven Justice, Ralph Hanna, and A. V. C. Schmidt, are also advocates of Ball's knowledge of B (as they must be), but as we have seen the textual indications in fact point toward the opposite conclusion. The case for B, if it is to stand, must thus rely entirely on much more impressionistic responses to the letters. *Þe Kynges sone of hevene*, maintains Schmidt, "is a characteristic group-genitive phrase little instanced outside the poem (B 18.320 //), and its conjunction here with the idea of 'paying for all' will recall the argument of B 18.340–41."[60] So it might in the minds of readers predisposed to believe Ball knew B, but others might take more convincing. The concept of Christ as son of the king of heaven is pervasive, and its expression via this grammatical construct is not as rare as Schmidt suggests; Richard Rolle, too, refers to "Criste, the keyng sonn of heven."[61] Whatever affinities the phrase *schal paye for al* has with the argument of lines 340–41, "*Ergo* soule shal soule quyte and synne to synne wende / And al þat man haþ mysdo, y man wole amende," seem to me very general as well. In this phrase George Kane finds a different echo, of "Ac for þe pore y shal paye, and puyr wel quyte here travaile" (B 11.195), which is even more distant.[62]

Kane cites another parallel, between *sekeþ pees, and hold ȝou þerinne* and

Quod Consience to alle cristene tho, "my consayl is to wende
Hastiliche into unite and holde we us there.
Preye we þat a pees were in Peres berne þe Plouhman" (B 19.355–57)

which seems more promising.[63] The appearance of Ball's injunction immediately after the *dowel* tag seems to offer support—but, again, all this is also in Psalm 33:15, "recede a malo et *fac bonum, quaere pacem* et persequere eam" ("turn away from evil and *do good*: seek after peace and pursue it").[64] Such phrases are everywhere in medieval devotional writings.

The same problem attends Steven Justice's extraordinarily influential assertion that Ball knew a particular passage of the B version. Attempting to understand Walsingham's claim that Ball taught "that no one was fit for the kingdom of God who was born out of wedlock," Justice cites Wit's invective against those born out of wedlock: "Aȝen dowel they do yvele and þe devel plese" (B 9.199): "Here are Ball's bastards."[65] Yet the teaching that those born out of wedlock are unfit for the kingdom of God is biblical: "A mamzer [KJV: bastard], that is to say, one born of a prostitute, shall not enter into the church of the Lord, until the tenth generation" (Deut. 23:2).[66] In any case, this line appears in A as well (10.213),[67] so the reasons for Justice's nomination of B as Ball's source cannot be found here. But the assumption that the line's B rather than A appearance incited Ball prompts Justice to claim that "Ball found the epithet that dictated" the execution of Simon Sudbury, the archbishop of Canterbury, in Wit's claim that "*Proditor est prelatus cum Juda qui patrimonium christi minus distribuit*" ("He is a *traitor like Judas*, that prelate who too scantily distributes the patrimony of Christ" [B 9.94α]). And on the basis of this second assumption he indulges in a third, claiming that the rebel letters revise Langland's portrayal of the poem as inquiry, as an endless quest, in passus 8, 12, and 20.[68]

As Justice grants, however, anyone looking to connect bastardy, disendowment, and capital punishment, as does Ball, would find little in

Langland.[69] What he does not acknowledge is that great riches, of the highest authority, await discovery in the chapters leading up to Moses' invective against bastards:

> Thou shalt bring forth the man or the woman, who have committed that most wicked thing [i.e., idolatry], to the gates of thy city, and they shall be stoned. . . . Thou mayst not make a man of another nation king, that is not thy brother. And when he is made king, he shall not multiply horses to himself. . . . He shall not have many wives, that may allure his mind, nor immense sums of silver and gold. . . . But the prophet, who being corrupted with pride, shall speak in my name things that I did not command him to say, or in the name of strange gods, shall be slain. (Deut. 17:5,15–17; 18:20)

St. Paul strikes a very similar chord in warning that "neither fornicators, nor idolaters, nor adulterers, nor the effeminate, nor liers with mankind . . . shall possess the kingdom of God" (1 Cor. 6:9–10; cf. Eph. 5:5). Langland's own interest in this is suggested by his citation, just before the passage Justice quotes, of 1 Corinthians 7:1–2, "*Bonum est ut unusquisqui uxorem suam habeat propter fornicacionem*" (19.40). Isabel Davis nominates this letter as a likely source for Wit's discussion of marriage.[70] And Bromyard's citation of both the Deuteronomic and Pauline materials in the entry on *luxuria* in his *Summa Praedicantium* is especially suggestive.[71]

Ball is not speaking Langland, then; rather, both Ball and Langland are speaking St. Paul, most likely via a conduit such as Bromyard. Invectives against sexual misconduct pervaded medieval religious and ethical thought. A parallel debate about the relationship between Ball's letters and *Piers Plowman* will bring my objection into focus. At least three commentators have argued that the absence of wrath from the lists of the deadly sins in both Ball's first letter and *Piers Plowman* A, but not B, "points towards the A version as that known to the participants in the rebellion."[72] To this Jill Mann objects, "given the familiarity of the sevenfold scheme, it is difficult to see why Ball would have shown so slavish an adherence to the A text, especially since the six-line poem on the sins does not show any verbal influence from *Piers Plowman*."[73] Just so—and given the familiarity of Deuteronomy, Paul's letters, and sermonic materials, it is difficult to see why Ball would have shown so slavish an adherence to the B text, especially since the sermon on bastards does not show any verbal influence from *Piers Plowman*.

John Ball's writings have turned into a hothouse of allusions, in which evidence keeps sprouting without having established roots in an explanation of *why* Ball, who had long been preaching and taunting his ecclesiastical adversaries, would suddenly need *Piers Plowman* for such bedrock ideas as "doing well." Thus while Richard Firth Green cites *do wel and bettre* as "confirmation, if any were needed, that this is a conscious Langlandian allusion,"[74] those not as invested in identifying Ball's reading of the poem could just as easily see it as a conscious allusion to St. Paul's "both he that giveth his virgin in marriage, doth well; and he that giveth her not, doth better" (1 Cor. 7:38), the verse in which Isabel Davis finds Langland's inspiration for Wit's definition of Dowel. We ourselves might do well to heed Margaret Aston's revival of an earlier approach to the topic:

> "Lokke that Hobbe robbyoure be wele chastysed. . . ." Of course it was possible to apply the words to Robert Hales, but the alliterative Rob or Hob Robber was an ancient and familiar figure. Should we not be wary (*pace* today's literary scholars) of assuming that Piers Ploughman, who appears alongside Hob Robber, is a reference to Langland's poem? The words "do well and better" scarcely prove the point, since "Do well" had its proverbial context long before the poem appropriated it. The figure of Piers the honest ploughman may already have been an alliterative type (as much as Tom Tinker, Miles Miller and Piers Potter) called on by John Ball as by Langland for their different purposes. This is an unfashionable view, but it had the support of C. S. Lewis.[75]

In light of the strength of her objection, and of the fact that the only items with strong Langlandian resonances appear in A and are traceable back to Bromyard, St. Paul, and the like, attempts to depict Ball as a sophisticated reader of the B version go far beyond what the evidence will support. The most these letters tell us is that some catch-phrases from A might have made their way somehow to Ball; and they might not even tell us that.

## Conclusion: The Earliest Circulation of *Piers Plowman*

It is not impossible that Ball or Chaucer could have read the B version by c. 1380, just much more likely that they knew A, if any version at all. The quick promulgation of C (if indeed it is to be dated to c. 1390)—an average of almost one copy a year in each line of transmission, culminating in the surviving fourteenth-century manuscripts—underscores, as does the A line before it, just how shadowy the pre-1390 B tradition is by comparison. Over the course of this book the belief in an integral pre-1390 *Piers Plowman* that looked something like our modern "B version" will only recede farther from the realm of reasonability. This statement perhaps appears more provocative than it ought, for my argument will be simply that *"Piers Plowman* B" as studied today is the product of conflation of the "ur-B" version that Langland wrote c. 1378 (whatever the extent of its circulation) and the earliest stages of C, and as such was representative of a major mode of the poem's production in the era of C's initial dissemination, which, crucially, was also the era of Bx. Because critics have always assumed a correlation between the "shapes" of certain of the surviving texts and the "versions" (i.e., what Langland wrote), the textual criticism of *Piers Plowman*, while among the richest and most advanced in English studies and perhaps beyond, remains in some ways in its early stages. Until it confronts the possibility that Bx, like so many of its chronological peers, was conflated by C materials, even if only to reject it, Langland criticism, not just its textual subfield, will be based more on faith than on evidence.

# Scribal Conflation, Convergent Variation, and the Invention of *Piers Plowman* B

The archetype of all surviving B copies, as we saw in the Preface, concludes with a rubric expecting a further, twenty-first passus: an odd error resulting from contamination by a C manuscript, in which the rubric worked perfectly well as an explicit. These few pen-strokes in manuscripts L and R thus have enormous consequences in that they identify the moment of Bx's production as the era of conflation and conjoinment. The critical propensity for focusing only on authorial texts has led to an almost exclusive focus on the three versions, dated to the 1360s, 1370s, and 1380s respectively, but the landscape of *Piers Plowman* manuscripts in the final decade of the century was no respecter of that approach. This was when the desire for "completion" took hold: the energies that went into the compilations now found in the Ilchester Prologue, the BmBoCot group, and the TH²Ch group suggest that conflation and conjoinment might have been the normative modes of producing and reading the poem by this point in its history. Those who got their hands on a C version copy were set; the rest, though, sought out matter from here and there with the aim of compiling a complete *Piers Plowman*.

Might Bx itself have been the result of this desire for completion? If its very final inscription came from C, could the previous 850 lines, which are nearly identical in the surviving B and C traditions, have as well? And if that possibility is viable, as Chapter 4 will argue in detail, should we perhaps consider the idea that such conflation occurred in other locations? Say, those passages extant in only one of the B families? Over the 150-year editorial history of the poem, such ideas have never been mooted. As a result, many today might dismiss such speculations out of hand. Conflated texts always reveal their nature via signs of scribal officiousness, such skeptics might aver, citing George Kane's thorough analysis of manuscripts W, N, and K. And more to the point, no potential sources of conflation, other than those final two passus, present themselves. Yet such rejoinders are either just wrong, or the product rather than the foundation of critical approaches to the textual state of *Piers Plowman*. A three-pronged attack, comprising lemmatization, versioning, and the invocation of convergent variation at any signs of rupture to the existing paradigm, has buried the evidence that shows, contrary to that paradigm, that Bx was indeed affected by the C tradition to a far greater degree than the LR rubric indicates. In conclusion this chapter presents the bulk of my positive evidence that Bx, at one stage in its career as exemplar, was supplemented by lines and paragraphs of new C material, the existence of which has been obscured by its atomization into versions and then lemmas. In sum, an early scribe, like so many others between the Era of Ilchester in the 1390s and Sir Adrian Fortescue in 1532,[1] was jealous for the completeness of his copy, and thus turned to C materials to fill out the seemingly deficient manuscript in front of him.

## Officious Scribes, Inconsequential Transitions?

George Kane's chapter defining the character of *Piers Plowman* A, titled "Manuscripts and Versions," has never featured very prominently in Langland scholarship. C. L. Wrenn's early review, in effect saying that we knew all this before but there was no harm in Kane's rehashing of the material, is representative: "Though little that is positively new here emerges, there is real value in this thorough re-examination of the reasons which lead to the generally accepted conclusions." The "most important part of a very important Introduction," he continued, lay farther afield, in the following chapter on the classification of the manuscripts.[2] Yet insofar as it determined which manuscripts and which lections of those manuscripts would and would not be classified in any given volume of the Athlone edition, "Manuscripts and Versions" established the framework within which the Athlone enterprise, and all *Piers Plowman* criticism in its wake, would operate. In sum, it puts forth the idea that, once the obvious instances of scribal conflation among the versions are identified, the editor is left with the authorial versions: here, "*Piers Plowman* A," but by implication the other two versions, B and C, as well.

The local problem is the inclusion in A-version witnesses of additional lines or passages corresponding to matter from the B and C versions. Kane argues "that these seven manuscripts received this B or C material, and their present shapes, through scribal compilation, and that they are actually contaminated and augmented copies of the A version."[3] The main offenders are the Duke of Westminster's manuscript (W; 95 lines at twenty-eight points), National Library of Wales MS 733B (N; about 150 lines at twenty-one points, many shared with W), and Adrian Fortescue's manuscript, Bodleian, MS Digby 145 (K; over 400 lines at thirteen points). Kane knows they are contaminated because they all bear the marks of "the officious copyist," who "tended to leave signs of his activity in the character of the text produced by his conflation." These signs "are happily unambiguous," revealing themselves "in the presence of both primitive and revised forms of the same passage; inappropriate or misplaced augmentation; in broken syntax; and in broken or inferior sense."[4]

Kane's first exhibit, where an irritated Holy Church identifies Meed in WN, provides a good snapshot of both the phenomenon and Kane's approach to it:

> In þe popis palis she is pryvei as my selfe;
> And so scholde sche nouȝt be for wrong was hir syre;
> Out of wrong sche wer to wroþer haile many.
> ***Talis pater talis filia.***
> **For shal nevre brere bere bery as a vyne**
> **Ne on a croked þorne kynde fygge waxe.**
> ***Arbor bona bonum fructum facit.***
> I ouȝt ben herre þan she for I come of a better.[5]

Kane identifies this as A 2.18–20, C 2.27α–29α (here in bold), A 2.21, and observes that in the C version A 2.20 "has been replaced by the point which C 2.28–29 are intended to drive home. Without this purpose, in WN, these lines are in the air. They can have been inserted only in ignorance of the local differences of meaning between the versions."[6] Since no poet could be ignorant of these differences, enter the officious scribe.

The chapter's insistent and antiscribal tone and close attention to example after example might lead some readers to conclude that conflation is always marked by signs of officiousness. But in fact Kane discusses only about one-third of the conflated passages, enough to imply that all of them represent scribal intrusions from other versions.[7] Many others are perfectly smooth. For example, Kane cites nine of MS N's twenty-one sites of intrusion as officious. Of the remainder, five consist simply of the Latin found in the C version, and two are single lines in the list of companions who enter the pub during Gluttony's confession (added as well by MSS VH(EA)MH³); none of these affects syntax.⁸ That leaves five sites of intrusion, totaling over sixty lines, about which Kane says nothing. All of them consist of English additions integrated seamlessly into received A.

Immediately after Holy Church's enhanced identification of Meed in MS N, that document alone smoothly includes C 2.31–41α at the juncture of A 2.21–22. On one end line 21 is equivalent to C 2.30—indeed it would be just as accurate to say that N is simply continuing the conflation begun with line 27α⁹—and on the other, both A 2.22 and C 2.42 begin with the phrase "Tomorewe worþ." Equally straightforward is the first conflation common to W and N:

> "Þu doted daff!" quod sche, "dul are þi wittis.
> **For litel lerestow I leve of latyn in þi ȝowþe:**
> *Heu mihi quia sterilem duxi vitam Juvenilem.*
> It is a kynde knowyng þat kenneþ in þin herte . . ."¹⁰

Kane identifies this as A 1.129 and 130 into which are inserted (in bold) B 1.139–39α or C 1.140–40α. If these four lines were excerpted, though, they would simply be called either B 1.138–40 or C 1.139–41. Next, since lines 75 and 76 of A passus 3, "Ne bouhte none burgages, be ȝe ful certayn. / Ac Mede þe mayde þe mayre a bisowte," are equivalent to C 3.85 and 115 respectively, it was very simple for N, or the text in its line of transmission that initiated the conflation, to add that version's new intervening lines, 86–114. By the same token WN's addition of C 2.246–51 at the juncture of A 2.194–95 (= C 2.245, 252), too, is seamless. Only a very willful scribe could have left signs of officiousness at any of these sites, given that Langland himself simply added new material at these junctures, which themselves survived the process of revision intact.

The most interesting such addition to MS N, where the friar-confessor asks Meed to engrave her name upon a window in the friary, shows that even where conflation is not a matter of simple addition, it could still be accomplished with no signs of officiousness. Here is the received A version of the episode, with the lines in question—to be replaced rather than added to in N—in bold:

"We han a wyndowe awurchynge wol stande us wel heye;
Wolde thow glase þe gable and grave ther thy name,
Sykir sholde thy soule be hevene to have."
**"Wiste I that," quod þe womman, "þere nis wyndowe ne auter**
**That y ne sholde make or mende, & my name writen**
**That uch segg shal se y am suster of ȝoure hous."**
Ac god alle good folk suche gravynge defendeth
And saith *Nesciat sinistra quid faciat dextera.* (A 3.47–54)

The passage appears in National Library of Wales 733B thus:

"We have a wyndowe iwrouȝt stant us wel hiegh;
Woldestow glase þe gable & grave þere þi name,
Siker scholde þi soule be hevene to have."
**"Wist I þat," quod þat womman, "I wolde nouȝt spare**
**For to be ȝour frende, frere, & faile ȝow nevre**
**Wil ȝe love lordis þat lecherie haunteþ**
**And lakkeþ nouȝt ladies þat loveþ wel þe same.**
**It is a freelte of flesche—ȝe fynde it in bokys—**
**And a course of kynde whereof we comyn alle;**
**Who may scape þe sklaunder, þe skaþe is sone amendid;**
**Hit is synne of þe sevene sonnest relest.**
**Have mercy," quod Mede, "of men þat it haunte**
**And I schal kevre ȝour kirke, ȝour closter do make,**
**Wowes do whiten & wyndowes glasen,**
**Do pointin & purtraye & pay for þe makyng**
**Þat evry segge schal seen þat I am sistre of ȝour hous."**
But god to alle good folke suche gravyng defendeþ:
*Nesciat sinister quid faciat dexter.*[11]

This instance appears to be N's sole conflation from the B tradition, as this is equivalent to Kane and Donaldson's B 3.51–63 (though only one of the two B families attests it, the other instead having a spurious version of lines that look like the ones N replaces, A 3.50–52). As such this will become very prominent later in the chapter, but for now the point is that N, whatever the source of his conflation, does not fall prey to the temptation of including both primitive and revised forms of the same passage. Since both the a-verse at the site of substitution and the entire line with which the passage ends are identical in both texts, the sin was not too difficult to avoid, but many readers would come away from Kane's chapter assuming that scribes left signs of their incompetence whenever the opportunity presented itself.

This is not a criticism of Kane's methodology or conclusion, simply a reminder that his point was local: where manuscripts that otherwise attest the A version have passages in common with C, and where the inclusion of many of those passages results in inconsequence, repetition, broken sense and the like, it is fair to conclude that these manuscripts' shapes are the results of scribal rather than authorial behavior. He was not arguing that all conflations bear signs of officiousness. No student of the poem's production can dismiss conflation from consideration just because a passage is smooth. After c. 1390, conflation is always a possibility. It comes to its fullest fruition in the appearance, a few decades later, of Huntington MS Hm 114 (Ht), which combines matter from all three major textual traditions,[12] but there is no reason to exclude Bx from consideration of its workings.

## Shapes and Versions

Ever since Walter Skeat divided *Piers Plowman*'s manuscripts into three authorial "versions," editors and critics have followed suit, assuming that each version comprised an integral body of manuscripts. It was clear that later texts combined matter from two or even three of these textual traditions, but no one seems to have considered the possibility that this could have occurred at the earlier stages as well. The versioning of the poem reached its apogee in the Athlone edition, which defined the A, B, and C texts by process of elimination followed by a leap of faith: once the editor identified the officious intrusions of the W, N, and K traditions, he would be left with "uniformity," assumed to equate to authorial integrity: "Among the more than fifty manuscripts preserving the work called *Piers Plowman* two distinct versions are handsomely attested by substantial numbers of copies of uniform shape. The remaining manuscripts have various shapes, but seventeen of them are distinguished by the common possession of some 400 lines not found in the other two versions."[13] The "two distinct versions of uniform shape" are of course B and C, while the 400 lines shared by the remaining manuscripts identify them as witnesses to A, which take "various shapes" via acts of conflation and the additions of C conclusions in W, N, K, and the TH²Ch group.

Although the classification of any given witness to the poem by its "shape" appears to be merely preliminary to the more rigorous work of critical editing, it is in fact a compromised pre-determiner of that editing's outcomes. The "uniform shape" attested by B and C manuscripts is very broadly defined: B manuscripts feature a Prologue and 20 passus; C manuscripts, a Prologue and 22 passus; and each, a series of passages not in the other. But given that the surviving B tradition did not assume its current "shape" until conflation had already begun, and that conflation did not always leave signs of its presence, it remains unclear on what grounds Kane assumes that the shape of B is solely the product of authorial activity. On the one hand, "shapes" are determined by the character of a manuscript's passages; on the other, "shapes" predetermine the character of a manuscript's passages. Here is a major dilemma that has not figured in Langland criticism precisely because that criticism's methodologies bury the evidence that shows it to be so deeply misleading.

The prior classification of the evidence into three independent groups produced some decidedly odd results, which perhaps should have raised the alarm a while ago. For these "versions" interfered directly with the editors' own presentation and analysis of the surviving evidence. They stress, for instance, that with regard to *Piers Plowman* B 19–20 and C 21–22 "the manuscripts of the two traditions were treated as constituting two great families with an exclusive common ancestor, a single scribal B copy."[14] Yet such an approach calls for a single edition of those passus, with full display of collations, in the B edition. As it stands, that edition does not indicate whether Kane and Donaldson weighed or even had access to all the C readings, or to what degree C-editor George Russell bore responsibility for the readings printed in their B text. The famous conclusion to their Introduction claims:

> The apparatus supporting that text [sc. their B text] contains all material evidence for determining its original form afforded by the known B manuscripts other than S and Ht. How we have interpreted that evidence, and the evidence of the A and C versions bearing on it, has been laid wholly open to scrutiny in the preceding stages of this Introduction. Whether we have carried out our task efficiently must be assessed by reenacting it.[15]

But according to that same Introduction, the first of these statements is simply not true, for all "C" witnesses that include passus 21–22, too, are "known B manuscripts." The absence of the C readings from the collation thus means that users cannot reenact the editors' task, or even be sure which set of editors' tasks they cannot reenact, with regard to those important lines. Russell and Kane's edition of C does not address this problem. The power accorded the "versions" enables the predetermined categories of "B" and "C" to obscure the workings of the editorial process, the display of which is what in this passage the editors justifiably claim to be the single indispensable characteristic of any good critical edition (and which in nearly every other way the Athlone edition epitomizes).

The assumption that the surviving "shapes" correspond to the authorial "versions" also both enacted and brought about two major problems with the circumstances in which editors have classified manuscripts by shared error. The first comes into focus via Talbot Donaldson's description of the circularity of manuscript classification in the service of stemmatic editing:

> if an editor has to be able to distinguish right readings from wrong in order to evolve a stemma which will in turn distinguish right readings from wrong *for* him, then he might as well go on using this God-given power to distinguish right from wrong throughout the whole editorial process, and eliminate the stemma. The only reason for not doing so is to eliminate the appearance—not the fact—of subjectivity: the fact remains that the whole classification depends on purely subjective choices made before the work of editing begins.[16]

The force of this objection is mitigated, with regard to *Piers Plowman* at least, by the fact that the "work of editing," whether via the construction of a stemma or a reading-by-reading critical judgment as Donaldson advocates, occurs within the parameters of a group of readings—those of the "version" being edited—that are selected even before any of them is judged authorial. Whether one edits "B" via recension or in the Kane-Donaldson manner hardly matters if the object of editing has shaped rather than been determined by the manuscript readings.

## Convergent Variation and Conjectural Emendation

An even more pressing problem brought about by this collapsing of "shapes" into "versions" concerns the explanatory power of "convergent variation" beyond its justifiably vast reaches. It was among Kane's greatest achievements to demonstrate the pervasiveness of this phenomenon. The witnesses share so many agreements of error that a substantial proportion could not have arisen via descent from a common ancestor. For instance, while the A-version manuscripts V and H share some 230 exclusive common errors, "against the variational group VH must be set four groups in which H appears with another manuscript than V," Kane points out, "and four groups in which V appears with another manuscript than H, comprising together more than 120 agreements which, if VH is genetic, must be random."[17] These agreements of each manuscript with witnesses other than its partner, that is, came about not because of mutual descent from a common ancestor, but from either coincident substitution, which "occurred because every piece of text in its context contained inducements to certain classes of substitution, from its content or language or metrical form," or consultation of another copy, or memorial contamination, in which "any part of the text he had so far copied, or any part of the whole text if he was copying it for a second time, could intrude in the system of messages from eye to brain to hand and substitute another reading."[18]

Convergent variation had a controversial and dramatic effect on Langland scholarship: the replacement of manuscript testimony with "conjectural emendation" as the driving force, psychologically if not substantially, of the editing of its canonical text. The classification of the manuscripts, writes Kane, while "removing the last grounds for belief that a genealogy of these manuscripts serviceable for recension could be recovered," nevertheless has "positive results": "Clearly, if tendencies of variation could be established, the knowledge of those tendencies would afford means of distinguishing original from unoriginal variants where originality might not otherwise be immediately apparent."[19] The editor, armed with the knowledge of the types of errors to which scribes were prone—ones that result in the phenomenon of convergent variation—must judge every reading on its own merits.

Most users of Kane's edition of A have agreed that this is a very productive approach to a version witnessed by so many divergent manuscripts and groups. Kane and Donaldson's application of this methodology to B, though, has taken on an alarming hue for many users.[20] For one, the editors, via comparison of Bx with the often superior A and C texts, conclude that it "was markedly corrupt," much more so (some 600 readings) than ever suspected. They also engage in a number of other comparisons—superior A with inferior BC readings; poor BC readings with their sense of what Langland would have written; faulty B passages with C's attempts at repair—that "also establish that, notwithstanding its superior originality at those points, th[e] B manuscript used by Langland for his second revision was a corrupt scribal copy" as well.[21] Taken together, the inability to grant any single manuscript more authority than others and the corruption of both Bx and its ancestor, the C reviser's B manuscript, "combine to discredit manuscript authority: relative strength of attestation is altogether unreliable, and unanimous attestation even in several traditions by no means surely reliable evidence of originality."[22]

Thus the rise of "conjectural emendation," and of an extraordinary and lively controversy that put the textual and editorial traditions of *Piers Plowman* in the center of critical consciousness, even beyond the realm of Middle English studies.[23] Everyone knows that the Athlone Langland is a figure far removed from the readings found in the extant B manuscripts, a great poet come to life only through extensive editorial ministrations. But while in most respects the editors and their critics sit on opposite sides of such issues, these disparate parties are united in their silent assumption that the surviving shapes of the manuscripts, whatever the nature of their lections, are *not* in need of conjectural emendation. Insofar as critics have rejected what they see as the Athlone edition's unmerited disdain of scribes' roles in the production of the received texts, it might seem surprising that they have not challenged the editors to consider the possibility that scribes played a role in creating the surviving "shapes" at the archetypal stages of copying. Instead, the edition's fiercest opponent advocates comparison of manuscripts "by lines and readings rather than by broad narrative shape,"[24] and others seek either to increase the amount of integral authorial material assigned to Bx or to accept the authorial status of the versions as absolutes and simply reorder them.[25] To allow that Bx might have been conflated would have been to give away the game, since the acceptance of that idea would result in even larger-scale emendation than already had (in their judgment) violated the received text.

Critics' almost exclusive focus on Athlone-style conjectural emendation of lections has skirted a more pressing point: the circumscription of the entire discussion about the textual status of *Piers Plowman* by arbitrarily determined "shapes" assumed, on the basis of faith rather than evidence, to correspond to the authorial texts.

## The Power of the Alphabet

The heated controversy attending the Athlone edition of *Piers Plowman* was focused on two quite separate categories of text. Most criticism fell into line with an editorial dispensation that takes the individual lection as its primary body of evidence, from Robert Crowley's observation that "the Englishe is according to the time it was written in, and the sence somewhat darcke" to the modern penchant for glossaries and concordances.[26] Within the editions themselves, this emphasis is manifested in the process of lemmatization, of listing variants term by term after the appearance of the endorsed reading— the lemma—in the apparatus as the bottom of the page. At the other end of the spectrum is the focus on large-scale versions. In choosing this arena as her battleground, Jill Mann figured, magnanimously if arbitrarily, that she ought to abandon the usual lection-based mode of argumentation: "I have tried to avoid the charge of special pleading by ignoring these individual manuscript variations, and confining myself to the texts established by Kane and Donaldson on criteria that have nothing to do with the theory I wish to support."[27]

These two categories are undoubtedly foundational. Without the concept of versions the student of *Piers Plowman* would drown beneath all the manuscript variation. And Langland often revised lection-by-lection, underscoring the fact that this procedure is necessary to the editing of *Piers Plowman*. But while necessary, it is not sufficient.[28] Lost between these two extremes is the paragraph-length passage. Langland also wrote out new passages on separate sheets to be added to the preexisting text, the material existence of which can easily be forgotten via the exclusive focus on the lemma and the version. And the possibility that, say, new C passages might have played a role in the production of Bx can be tested only with the greatest difficulty, given the combination of that lemmatization and the predetermination of what constitutes the "versions."[29] If, say, a C-version manuscript agreed with a B-version family for entire paragraphs, the evidence would be almost entirely obscured by these two approaches.

The materials Mann adduces to mount her case will bring home the point and lead us into entirely new directions. She argues that the relative absence of both Latin and sexual materials in A suggests that Langland revised his longer B and C versions for a provincial, non-Latinate, and prudish readership. Mann is unable to "believe that Langland was a prosaic, sexually prudish, socially conservative youth, who was suddenly liberated into a creative, sexually explicit, socially radical middle age by his prolonged meditation on Latin biblical texts."[30] Among her main exhibits is "Meed's plea to the friar who gives her confession to take an easy attitude to lechery, since it is a 'cours of kynde' (B 3.52–62); A omits this (cf. A 3.50–52), presumably because an unsophisticated audience might not see the irony here and might be led astray by Meed's arguments."[31] This passage is familiar to us as among those that National Library of Wales MS 733B attests in its A portion, in fact the only one that could have been from "B" rather than C. The quotation marks are necessary, though, because it appears only in the W-M family of B, with the RF family instead attesting a spurious version of A's three lines.

Mann's other major example of the omission of sexual material from B to A follows the identical pattern of W-M/N² agreement (where N² signals the C material in NLW 733B) against RF/A, suggesting that something much different from what she imagines is going on beneath the level of the "versions." She cites A 10.197–204 vs. B 9.176–91, in which "A diverges from B as B begins to talk about avoiding lechery by using one's 'wepen kene' in marriage (185), and then follows this exhortation to vigorous marital sex with two lines of Latin," rejoining B at 189.[32] Again, Mann's decision to ignore the apparatus prevented her from noticing that the RF family, too, does not attest these lines.[33] And while the late appearance of Russell and Kane's edition of C delayed any hope of discovery that N² happens to agree with W-M against received C for this entire passage, she almost certainly would not have noticed anyway. Not just because of her decision to ignore that body of evidence, but also because of the combination of an assumption that the versions were integral and the burial of the evidence in an avalanche of lemmata at the bottom of the page. Here is C 10.283–89 as printed by Russell and Kane, followed by N²'s relevant readings as presented in that edition's apparatus, isolated from the other manuscript variants there recorded:[34]

> And every maner seculer man þat may nat contynue
> Wisely go wedde and war þe fro synne;
> That lecherye is a lykyng thynge, a lymȝerd of helle.
> And whil þou art ȝong and ȝep and thy wepene kene
> Awrek the þerwith on wyfyng, for godes werk y holde hit:
> *Dum sis vir fortis ne des tua robora scortis;*
> *Scribitur in portis, meretrix est janua mortis.*
> Ȝe þat han wyves ben war and worcheth nat out of tyme
> As Adam dede and Eve, as y whil er tolde.

**283** maner] man DSN². man] *om* DAN². nat] now N².
**284** þe] hym DN². synne] DGN²; þat synne [*rest of MSS*].
**285** That . . . a(2)] For lecherye & lykyng is N².
**286** And] *om* N². and ȝep] *om* N².

**287** Awrek] Wrek SN². þer] *om* EN². on] *om* N². for . . . hit] ȝif þou wil
ben excused N².

**288** ȝe þat] Whan ȝe N². wyves] wyved N². nat . . . of] in N².

**289** As] Nouȝt as N². dede] *om* N². as . . . tolde] whan caym was
engendrid N².

In the governing paradigm of *Piers Plowman* textual studies, anyone who
might notice, say, that N²'s *now* for received *nat* at C 10.283 brings it into line
with Kane and Donaldson's B 9.182—who, that is, has a memory capacious
enough to notice this, or goes to the trouble of isolating this single variant
among thousands and comparing it to the reading of a version whose edition
was published twenty-two years earlier—would almost certainly attribute the
agreement to the workings of coincidence, the most common of the three forms
of convergent variation. The power of versions at one end and lemmata at the
other would enable the revelation of this pattern only to the most suspicious
and patient reader of the fine print spread across all three Athlone editions.

A reader who continues to cross-check the apparatuses for the lines and
passages not in RF against those given in the A and C editions, though, will
discover that the pattern of W-M/N² agreements against RF/A at those sites
is not confined to the two that Mann had unknowingly discussed. It includes
a series of lines leading up to Wit's exposition on sexual sins, and a handful
of lines just after it. The chart here summarizes the situation in those places
where A is extant. The received paradigm of "versions" has attempted to ac-
count for RF's "omission" of passages also lacking in A (those marked "[noth-
ing]" in the left column) as either the result of eyeskip or as those B-revision
passages' attestation on loose slips of paper that were absent from Bx when the
RF scribe was copying.[35] Whatever the merits of either approach, they were
put forth before N² of C's perfect filling of the void left by RF of B came to
light, a fact neither of the received approaches can accommodate.

| A; RF of B | W-M of B; N² of C | Rest of C |
|---|---|---|
| A 3.50–52; RF spurious ll. | B 3.51–63 | C 3.56–67 |
| [nothing] | B 8.14–17 | C 10.14–17 |
| [nothing] | B 9.163–64 | C 10.254–55 |
| A 10.190; RF traces in B172 | B 9.169 (after 171) | C 10.270 |
| A 10.194–96; RF spurious ll. | B 9.173–75 | C 10.275–77 |
| [nothing] | B 9.182–88 | C 10.283–89 |
| [nothing] | B 9.202–6 | C 10.301–5 |

But if the versions do not accord with the passages that supposedly make up those versions, perhaps it is time to strip those versions of some of the power they have held for so long over Langland studies. My proposal is that, while the two "B" families, RF and W-M, did indeed share access to the identical exemplar, Bx, the passages from this chart were not integral to it. Neither were a few others, including a major instance that is the subject of Chapter 3. When the scribe of the W-M ancestor copied Bx, this material had been added on loose sheets from the first draft of Langland's C materials, as represented now almost exclusively by $N^2$; by the time the scribe of the RF ancestor made his copy, though, it was no longer there, and would be subject to final C revisions. Where the passages were new to C, RF read nothing, since B here had not yet been supplemented and still agreed with the earlier A version.

The most telling aspect of this phenomenon occurs where the lines *replaced* material unchanged from A to B, as in Meed's plea to the friar in passus 3. Here it seems clear that the equivalent lines in Bx had been marked in that document as superseded. The RF scribe thus knew that the matter in front of him was stale, but, lacking access to the fresh lines, decided to fudge it by writing out spurious lines instead.[36] This explains how A/Bx's verses:

> "Wiste y þat," quod þe womman, "there nis wyndowe ne auter
> That y ne sholde make or mende, and my name writen
> That uch seg shal se y am sustre of ȝoure house" (A 3.50–52)

became this in RF:

> "Wist I þat," quatȝ mede, "þere nys wyndow no wowȝ
> Þat I ne wolde make and amende it with of myne
> And my name write openliche þerInne
> That ech a segge shal see I am suster to ȝow alle."[37]

No one else has ever explained the spurious nature of these RF passages: the unavailability of $N^2$'s readings before 1997 prevented readers from recognizing that all their appearances coincide with $N^2$ agreements with W-M, and the lemmatization of those readings in the edition finished off the job.

If passus 3 and 9 of B were the only locations where RF read gobbledegook for lines in which W-M and $N^2$ agreed, it might seem just possible that the passages unavailable to the RF scribe were loose B-era revisions of original A material. But the pattern continues well after A is no longer extant, meaning, first, that this *is* a pattern, not coincidence upon coincidence, and second, that these must be C-era revisions of ur-B matter.

| RF of B | W–M of B; N² of C | Rest of C |
|---|---|---|
| [nothing] | B 12.169 | C 14.109 |
| [nothing] | B 15.533–69 (misplaced by W–M) | C 17.194–232, 250–51 |
| three spurious lines | B 16.270–73 | C 18.286–89 |

The crucial instance here is the third, where W–M/N² read

> "Allas!" y saide, "þat synne so longe shal lette
> The myhte of goddes mercy that myhte us alle amende."
> Y wepte for his wordes; with þat saw y another
> Rappliche renne forth þe riȝt way he wente[38]

where RF has

> "Allas," thouȝte I þo, "þat is a longe abydynge,"
> And sued hym for he softe ȝede
> Þat he toek us as tit ac trewly to telle.[39]

The W–M/N² material here cannot attest "new" B matter intended to re-place A lines. This pattern thus took effect much later than the A > B revision. In short, the situation is not that N² has "B" lines and passages, but the other way around: W–M took on passages totaling eighty-one lines new to the early draft of C as recorded now only in N². MS N²'s status as witness to an earlier draft of C is also apparent in its attestation of sixty-four readings also in Bx through B 18/C 20, and in its agreement with W–M for another ninety-three readings where RF agree with Cx. This body of 157 individual lections had simply not yet been revised to final C form by the time Nx (as I term the an-cestor of N² that was responsible for these readings) was produced, while RF later got hold of the final C revisions—a matter for later chapters.[40]

What of earlier proposals of N²'s "B-character" readings, such as Russell and Kane's that they may be "correction[s] from a pre-archetypal C copy," given that "N²'s exemplar or a close ancestor originated where consultation of other copies was easy,"[41] or A. V. C. Schmidt's and Ralph Hanna's that they attest contamination of $N^2$ or its ancestor by a manuscript from the W-M tradition?[42] These are explanations not of the problem—that Nx and W-M agree *overwhelmingly where RF is absent or spurious*—but of half of it: that Nx and W-M agree. Even there, they address only a small proportion of that half, as none of them seems aware of the extent of the supposed contamination. Schmidt, for instance, does not even cite the agreements we have been discussing, on the grounds that RF's absence constitutes "zero evidence" as to the source of $N^2$'s assumed contamination.[43] That is to assume what remains to be proven—and what the very fact of RF's absence shows *cannot* be proven, since it did not occur. Take, for instance, the fact that the two B-tradition groups, W-M and RF, share 95 percent of their readings (which is what makes them both "B-tradition" groups after all). What this means is that contamination of a C manuscript by a witness to either group would reveal its source as W-M or RF in particular, rather than "B" in general, only about 5 percent of the time.[44] In other words, in a normal situation in which a manuscript of the W-M tradition contaminated Nx or $N^2$ with 250 readings, only about a dozen would be identifiable as from that group and not RF. Yet the number in the situation we are discussing is instead 186, or 74 percent, *fifteen times* greater than we would expect in a situation of random contamination, and far more than chance would allow. If such objections to my argument are to be taken seriously, they need to account for the problem of RF's divergence from Nx/W-M rather than continuing to ignore it. The findings of Chapter 3 below will make that task all the more difficult.

Where does National Library of Wales MS 733B, the document itself, fit in all this? The fact is that its own history is not a main player of our story; it is its text, which surely is some generations descended from that of Nx, that is so important. Still, given its unique role in *Piers Plowman's* textual history, we will want to know as much as possible about this manuscript. Ian Doyle describes it as "on poor membrane and by a clumsy bastard anglicana with perfunctory decoration, of uncertain origin and date, probably not far into the fifteenth century, perhaps where better could not be done or by someone who could not afford better."[45] My preliminary dialectal analysis suggests Warwickshire as that unfortunate location,[46] and in the fifteenth century one John (?)Staunton, chaplain of (?)Rothendell, inscribed his name in it some four times.[47] It now lacks its opening and concluding quires, but the consistency with which it has about thirty lines a side, in gatherings of four, suggests to Kane that the manuscript originally contained another item prior to *Piers Plowman*.[48]

Besides these tantalizing hints of a fuller existence than it now has, though, National Library of Wales MS 733B has a single, and indispensable, item for us today: its remarkable text, the sole substantive witness to the stage of the C version's earliest life that I am calling Nx, which must have been produced some two or so decades earlier than this document itself, and that, I am proposing, contained loose sheets of new "C" materials that we have mistaken for poetry integral to "B." At this stage my proposal is still new, and might seem unduly difficult. But, as Kane said about his discussion of MSS W, N, and K, "To reject an explanation because it is complicated would suggest the improbability of complicated situations in the history of texts, which is manifestly false."[49] Such difficulty is more a function of that newness, and of the universal assumption that Kane's "Manuscripts and Versions" chapter establishes rather than assumes a relationship between uniformity of shape and authorial integrity, than of anything inherent in the proposal. The idea that an exemplar was supplemented with material from another version is so uncontroversial as to be banal. Even the idea that loose sheets of early C matter were in circulation has already gained firm support, well before $N^2$'s potential role was known: around the time of Bx's production, Scribe D or one of his predecessors in the line of transmission of his Ilchester copy, too, seems to have had access to such material, whose affiliations suggest strongly that it might descend from Nx itself.[50] And Kane could be speaking for me, once allowances for our different arguments are made, when he said, "Readers to whom its relative simplicity is not apparent are recommended to consider the assumptions which would be required by any hypothesis that the shape of W, or N, or K, for instance, is other than of scribal origin."[51]

As it happened, what Kane thought would be judged complicated was quickly accepted or indeed already assumed to be the case, as Wrenn's review quoted above confirms. Such has not, however, been true with Bx, which unlike any given A-version manuscript has taken on the presumption of integrity solely because it would later generate certain textual traditions. Yet Bx was only a manuscript of *Piers Plowman*, no more special in itself than MS t or the Ilchester manuscript or the generator of BmBoCot or any other one of the 1390s. No more special in itself, perhaps, but invaluable in its role as the site in which subsequent scribes, editors, and readers would invent the concept of "*Piers Plowman* B."

*Chapter 3*

# The Poison of Possession: B Passus 15

In a famous forty-line invective printed as B 15.533–69, Anima inveighs against the ill effects of the Donation of Constantine, the apocryphal act that was believed to have ceded the Lateran in Rome to the papacy.[1] This passage has long figured prominently in textual and editorial work on the poem, and its culminating lines (564–67), an explosive call for disendowment, have served as an important touchstone for studies of *Piers Plowman* and topics as diverse as Wycliffism, anticlericalism, Franciscanism, vernacularism, English historiography, and the politics of the C revision.[2] Here is the passage as it appears in National Library of Wales MS 733B, which although always deemed a witness to C here (sigil N[2]), in fact agrees with "B" at every point of divergence between the two versions, including the absence of four C-only lines ("B" agreements against C in bold):[3]

| 533/194 | It is rewþe to rede how **ryȝtwyse** men lyved, |
|---|---|
| | How þei defowled her flesche, forsoke here owne wille |
| | Fer fro kiþþe & fro kynne yvel cloþed ȝeden, |
| | Badly ybedded, no boke but **conscience**, |
| | Ne no rychesse but þe Rode to rejoysse hem Inne: |
| | *Absit nobis gloriari nisi in cruce domini nostri & c* |
| | And þo was **plente & pes** amonge pore & ryche, |
| | And now is rewþe to rede how þe rede noble |
| 540/201 | Is reverenced **ar þe rode**, **receyved** for þe worþier |
| 541/203 | Than cristes cros þat overcome deþ & dedly synne. |
| | And now is werre & wo, & who-so why axeþ: |
| | For coveitise aftre crosse; þe corone stant in golde. |
| | Boþe ryche & religiouse, þat rode þei honoure |
| | Þat in grotis is ygrave & in golde nobles. |

For coveitise of þat crosse **men** of holy kyrke

Shal **torne** as templeres did; þe tyme approcheþ faste.

**Wyte** [ʒe] nouʒt, gode men, how þo men honoured

549/211   More tresore þan trwþe? I dar not telle þe soþe;

550/213   Reson & riʒtfuldome þo religious **demed**.

Riʒt so þise **clerkys for** [ʒoure] coveitise ar **longe**

<Shal **deme** [d]os ecclesie & **ʒoure pride depose:**

*Deposuit potentes de sede.*>

ʒi[f] kniʒthode & kynde wit & **comune** conscience

To-gidre love lelly, leveþ it wel, **ʒe** bisshopes,

Þe lordechip of londes **for ever schal ʒe lese**,

And lyven as *levitici* **as** oure lorde ʒow techeþ:

*Per primicias & decimas.*

Whan Constantyne of **curteisye** holy kyrke dowed

Wiþ landes & leodes, lordeshipes & rentis,

An angel men herde an hiegh at Rome crye,

"[D]os ecclesie þis day haþ ydronke venyme

And [þo] þat have Petres power arn apoysoned alle."

A medycyne **mote** þerto þat **may** amende **prelatis**.

That sholde prey for þe pes, **possessioun** hem letteþ;

564/227   Take here londes, ʒe lordes, & lat hem lyve by dymes.

565/229   **ʒif** possessioun be poysen & inparfiʒt hem make

566/231   **Gode were** to deschargen hem for holychirche sake,

And purgen hem of **poysen** or more perel falle.

568/250   **ʒif** prestehod were parfyt **þe** peple scholde amende

Þat contrarye **Cristes** lawe & cristendome despise.

"It's the date, stupid": Anne Hudson's "first line of attack" with regard to the topic of "Langland and Lollardy" applies with particular force to this passage.[4] Whereas the most common assumption identifies the call to disendow the church in lines 564–67 with Wyclif's *De civili dominio* of c. 1377, Hudson instead finds "a clear echo here of the demands voiced by Ball and by Wat Tyler during the progress of the rebellion" of 1381.[5] Yet others have pushed the dating of these lines (and thus of B) in either direction, Aubrey Gwynn suggesting that they reflect "London opinion" of the winter of 1370–71, when "popular feeling against the clerical magnates and the *possessionati* was acute,"[6] and Pamela Gradon saying that Anima "would have been a credible participant in the famous scene depicted by Walsingham as taking place in

1385, when Parliament responded to Courtenay's refusal to accept lay taxa-
tion of the clergy *cum summa furia*, and demanded that the clergy should be
deprived of their temporalities as a remedy for their overweening pride."[7]

These associations of Anima's lines with major historical events of the four-
teenth century show that, whichever dating might be right, Langland criticism
urgently needs to come to terms with the passage's extraordinarily complicated
textual status. Even to call it "B 15.533–69," as we will see below, is to beg the
question. The treatment of this passage has already been the fulcrum of any edi-
tion of *Piers Plowman*, in the absence of any awareness that N[2] had anything to
do with the problem. The dissolution of that ignorance brings home the point
that the very identity of "the B version" as an integral poem available by c. 1380
is now at risk. My fundamental claim was laid out in Chapter 2: this forty-line
passage originated in the Nx line of transmission of C, not in B. Hudson's pro-
posal that this passage responds to the Rising of 1381, and even Gradon's quip
about Anima as a would-be parliamentarian c. 1385, are entirely reasonable.
But a comprehensive study of the textual problems of B 15 does more than just
re-affirm my general point. It also provides new evidence concerning the two
modes by which the C version left its mark on B: in the first stage loose sheets
went to Bx as copied by the scribe of the W-M ancestral copy; in the second,
a final set of revisions of individual lections were recorded in Bx as copied by
the RF scribe. The poem's transmission history was not one of three successive
versions, each of which resisted combination with other versions so as to make
later editors' jobs easier, succumbing only later to conflation and cross-versional
contamination. The early scribes of *Piers Plowman*, like their successors, saw
themselves as transcribing that vital poem, not a self-contained "version." This
is an unexceptionable idea, but it means we need to start over in our engage-
ment with the production and meaning of *Piers Plowman*.

## Misfolded Bifolia and Loose Sheets: B 15.533–69, c. 1955–2006

In his discussion of these lines Aubrey Gwynn noted that in Skeat's text, the
twenty-five line passage concluding with received 567, "And purgen hem of
poysen or more perel falle," "is in fact a digression, interrupting the main ar-
gument about the Church's mission to the heathen which is resumed" in the
following line. Gwynn allowed that "Langland was always liable to digress
from his theme under the stress of his emotions,"[8] but Kane and Donaldson,
perhaps prompted by his comment, saw here the "inconsequence, taking the

form of discourse interrupted for no apparent homiletic or dramatic purpose or effect, and with unsmoothed transitions" as a sign of a major pre-archetypal error in the transmission of the text.[9] Their rearrangement of the text from what they see as archetypal (501–3α, 533–69, 504–32, 570–613) to authorial (501–613) is the most dramatic and large-scale example of the editorial reconstruction of a corrupt archetype. And the error, they believe, already marred the pre-archetypal C reviser's B manuscript, since "the differences between the two versions have the appearance of attempts to improve a defective sequence, as if the C reviser had experienced the same sense of inconsequence which first led us to suspect textual corruption."[10]

If this diagnosis of "inconsequence" in the received text is accepted, as it has been by most if not all critics,[11] other questions arise: how did this inconsequence come about? Is the Athlone solution accurate? And how is the problem related to other problems in B passus 15? Kane and Donaldson's answer to the first of these is remarkable for being so imaginative and so *particular*: a shuffling of papers, with certain lines in certain places, during a scribe's coffee break, whose activities upon returning to his task are recoverable almost down to the level of the letter:

> The dislocation will have occurred through misfolding of the inner bifolium of a quire of the unbound exemplar after some of its content had been copied. This bifolium had 20 lines to a side, as follows:
>
> 496–513 / 514–32 / / 533–51 / 552–69.
>
> The scribe copied from it up to the Latin line 503α and then broke off. During the pause this bifolium, uppermost in his open, unbound copy, was disturbed. When replaced it was incorrectly refolded so that it now ran:
>
> 533–51 / 552–69 / / 496–513 / 514–32.
>
> Resuming work the scribe remembered that his place was on the first side of the middle fold of the uppermost quire. As this now lay he knew that he had not yet copied the first line and went ahead (possibly even encouraged by the presence in 533ff. of several themes which, from memory of 504–32, he was expecting). He copied two sides, to 569. Glancing at the third (496–513) he noticed the Latin *Querite et inuenietis* (503α), which he knew he had copied. He therefore did not copy 496–503α, but did copy 504–32; line 570, to which he then came, was on a new bifolium. If he signified his error by indicating the correct order whoever used his copy as an exemplar ignored or missed his signals.[12]

This is a brilliant reconstruction of the material circumstances of manuscript production, and Middle English studies is only the richer for it. It is also wild and far-fetched, not just because it relies on such an extensive series of particular events, but also, even more so, because it comes up against the uncomfortable fact that the RF family of B does not witness to Bx for precisely the lines that Kane and Donaldson deem erroneously located in that copy: "The fact that RF's omission is of the matter presumed dislocated is not significant," they claim: "there is no connexion between the events. RF's omission is typical of a scribe of their exclusive common ancestral tradition" and so forth.[13]

A problem even more pressing than this arose in Chapter 2: the fact that $N^2$, a supposed witness to C, happens to agree with W-M for precisely these forty lines. The immediate impulse among many critics might well be to maintain the current paradigm by saying that $N^2$ must have been contaminated by a manuscript of the W-M group for these lines. Those who would do so might welcome what appears to be support from Ralph Hanna and A. V. C. Schmidt, who, while remaining silent about this crucial passage, argue on other grounds that $N^2$ bears obvious signs of contamination by a manuscript of the W-M family.[14] The problem, as we saw in Chapter 2, is that the supposed source of the contamination is just *too* obvious: how is it that Nx or $N^2$ took on this manuscript's readings so overwhelmingly where an entirely unrelated manuscript was absent or spurious—for instance, this forty-line passage and not a line before or after? Are we to imagine that three separate scribes by coincidence faltered with regard to precisely the same forty lines, and did so only here? The eighteen lines of new C matter (17.233–49) somehow were available to the Nx scribe, who knew where they belonged and yet for some reason returned to his source of contamination for two, barely revised lines before then going back again to his normal exemplar, and in doing all this exhibited no signs of cobbling or confusion: how can this be?[15] The omission of the four new lines in C's version of the "poison of possession" passage is a real sticking point, too. As Donaldson said in 1955, with regard to RF's assimilation to A in passus 8 and 9, the middle passages of the program outlined in Chapter 2: "Once again we are faced with contamination, though in this case the contamination is not only downward, from the greater to the less, but entirely negative, from something to nothing. Whereas I might reluctantly accept the possibility of the former, I find it utterly impossible to accept the possibility of the latter"—which, though, is precisely what this proposal must do with regard to C 17.202, 212, 228, and 230.[16]

Donaldson's alternative proposal "is that none of these passages, including the B-version of the one in Passus 3 [lines 51–63], was in the original" exemplar used by the RF scribe—that is, in Bx—"but that they were introduced into the B-tradition later than the vast bulk of the text that we now have."[17] The status of our forty-line passage cements the case for him: it "is the most suspicious" of the longer passages not found in RF.

> It is a long passage to have been omitted accidentally, although it could represent the material contained on a single side. What is suspicious about it is particularly its relation to the C-text. In B the passage comprises lines 495–531 [KD 533–69 after their reconstruction]; in C, 17.194–251: up to C233 C and B are very similar, though C contains four additional single lines; C233–34 are parallel to B530–31 [568–69], as are C250–51, the intervening material having been added by C. The significant fact is that in C, as in RF, the line parallel to B494 [503] (C254) is immediately followed by the line parallel to B532 [504] (C255), as though no intervening passage ever existed. In C the passage equivalent to B495–531 [533–69] appears between the C-lines parallel to B489 [497] and 492 [501] (B490–91 [498–99] are omitted in C). This suggests either that in the B-tradition the passage was introduced late and inserted erroneously five lines later than the poet intended, or, perhaps more probably, that the poet wrote the passage after he had completed the context it now appears in in B, inserted it after B494 [503], and then later, in his C-manifestation, plucked it out and shifted it to the earlier position. It should be observed that in the latter case there is evidence that the poet himself thought of the passage as a movable insertion.[18]

In my judgment this analysis holds up much better than does either the misfolded-bifolium narrative that would replace it twenty years later or the proposal, first put forth by Skeat and achieving widespread attention finally in 1996–97, that it is, rather, RF whose unique passages are late additions, which simply ignores the force of this argument.[19] And in a major recent essay Robert Adams has repeated the idea that the lines "probably filled one side of an inserted, attached leaf" in Langland's B papers, and that the scribe of Bx either acquired this sheet after he had copied the surrounding passages or was confused by where to place them, "so he left the inserts as mere attachments, just as they had been in his exemplar."[20] In mounting this case Adams points out that many "heavily corrected" fair copies of other works (as he takes Bx to have been) "do, in fact, incorporate revisions by means of attached slips."[21]

This might seem to raise the possibility that this loose sheet of B revision matter somehow made it into the hands of the Nx scribe. Before adjudicating that proposal it is worth noting just how difficult is this idea that Bx was the repository of loose sheets of authorial material—difficult enough to prompt Donaldson to abandon this straightforward account of 15.533–69 in favor of one that renders these lines' absence from RF purely coincidental. There is no reason to think that Kane bullied him, or that the editors "could [not] have edited the B-version at all—other than as parallel [RF] and [W-M] texts— had they come to any other conclusion."[22] The Athlone editors' conviction that the C reviser's B manuscript was already corrupt reveals the problem. The 1955 essay describes Bx (Donaldson's "Copy 1") as "a single MS which was not the poet's autograph, but a rather hasty and inaccurate copy of it";[23] the 1975 edition, though, puts forth the compelling case (part but by no means all of which relies on what they see as C's response to the dislocated 533–69) that Bx was not a copy of the holograph, but one further stage, at the least, removed from that document. If Langland was already working on his C revisions before the production of Bx, he could not have added these "B" versions of these lines to a manuscript descended from the copy he was using for those very revisions.

Adams for his part does not face this particular problem, since he does not assent to the Athlone postulate of the corrupt C reviser's B manuscript. That alone will be a worry to those convinced by Kane and Donaldson's account, but even those sympathetic to his cause might well have difficulty agreeing with Adams that an explanation of B 15's production "simpler than Kane-Donaldson's" is "ready to hand," requiring only as an enabling assumption his hypothesis "that Bx was not entirely a fair copy and that the second half of Bx was extensively emended and corrected from an authorially revised scribal copy."[24] If I understand this right, this explanation is that (1) Langland wrote a B holograph, (2) a scribal copy was made, to which Langland added some passages, (3) the Bx scribe used that scribal copy as an exemplar, but he either decided not to copy the text on the loose sheets that Langland had added, not bothering even to sew them in his copy, or he finished before Langland added still further passages, which were now added to (but, again, not sewn into) the copy he made, (4) the W-M scribe made a final copy— the first in which Langland's lines were finally recorded. Meantime, the RF scribe's omission of the sequence of passages in passus 8 and 9 was a series of independent instances of eyeskip that only coincidentally happened to bring that text into line with the A version at each point, while passus 3's assimilation to A is also coincidental, being the result of self-censorship.[25]

This does not strike me as very simple, even aside from its appeal to large-scale coincidence. It would help if there were any precedent for the idea that authorial revision matter was added not to the holograph itself, to enable the production of a fresh transcription, but to the copy that had used the holograph as exemplar. Or for the concept that a scribe ever simply left loose authorial matter in that state rather than inscribing it into his copy. None of the examples Adams cites of manuscripts enhanced by revision matter comes close to either of these postulates, and I, for one, have trouble understanding the motivations of Langland in the first instance or the Bx scribe in the second. Added to the difficulty is that this narrative does not account for the indications, manifest in C-character rubric of MSS LR at the end of passus 20, that Bx was the product of the C era, in which case any proposal that places Bx in the earliest stages of B's authorial production falls apart.

And we still have not exhausted the list of problems posed by this approach. How plausible is the notion that such a loose sheet with lines 15.533–69 escaped RF's notice but ended up in the hands of a random C scribe— presumably a decade or so later—who replaced his forty-four C lines with these forty, but still retained his exemplar's new eighteen lines? How could it be that in doing so the Nx scribe created a perfectly smooth text where the only other scribe who copied them, W-M, marred his own text with inconsequence and unsmoothed transitions? As Adams says, any simpler explanation is obviously preferable. Fortunately, we do not need to create Bx in the image of Langland's B > C revision manuscript to find one. That revision copy, say Russell and Kane (who receive Adams's endorsement on this point), contained "well more than a dozen separate single leaves or bifolia of new material, interleaved or loose."[26]

This large collection of problems vanishes if the loose sheet was among the matter postulated by Russell and Kane, making its way to Bx. Again, there is powerful precedent even for the idea that such loose C matter circulated independent of its origins in Langland's revision copy. Derek Pearsall has proposed the possibility that the lines from C 9 in the Ilchester Prologue "were 'floating fragments,' attached by scribes where they thought fit," an idea Wendy Scase would later confirm by noting that Huntington 114 (Ht) attests this same variant material in its passus 6.[27] In my account, the sheet was part of the authorial exemplar available to the ancestral scribe Nx (the first post-holograph copy, which possibly turned into Cx upon further revision), confused the W-M scribe since there was no precise equivalent in his copy to the text's location in C, and had been removed or lost by the time RF copied Bx. An added benefit is that, because of the late origins of this postulated document, it does not demand an attempt to explain away the evidence of LR's C-character rubric as discussed in the Preface.

## Langland, St. Lawrence, and the Development of B 15/C 17, c. 1380–90

There is still additional support for my proposal, intriguing if indirect, which inheres in the indications that Langland originally envisioned the passage's home neither where W-M attests it (after 503α) nor at the 532/570 juncture (Kane-Donaldson, Schmidt), but at the 343α/344 juncture. The reason for the passage's absence from that location, I will argue, cannot be that a loose sheet of matter belonging to B was misplaced during the production of that version; and what is more, the C version's character in the equivalent locations strongly supports my claim that these forty lines were a part of its production, not B's.

First, a basic point: the arguments for the accepted location between 532 and 570 are thin on the ground, and all of them raise more problems than they solve. The only positive evidence that Kane and Donaldson offer for their reconstruction is that their 504-32 "would more naturally follow 501-30α" since both passages criticize prelates for not evangelizing—as both RF and C order the text, the "significant fact" adduced by Donaldson in 1955.[28] Yet it is equally true that in *all* forms in which this passage survives—C, RF, and W-M—the line parallel to 15.532 (C 17.282) is immediately followed by the line parallel to 15.570 (C 17.283), also as though no intervening passage ever existed, and making for a perfectly smooth—in my judgment, necessary— juxtaposition. The topic is St. Thomas Becket's role as model for bishops:

> 527   He is a forbisene to alle bisshopis and a briht myrrour
> And sovereynliche to suche þat of surie bereth þe name
> That huppe aboute in Ingelond to halewe men auters
> And crepe amonges curatours, confessen aȝeyn þe lawe:
> *Nolite mittere falcem in messem alienam.*
> Many man for cristes love was martired in Romayne

532    Or eny cristendoem was knowe þere, or eny croos honoured.
570    Every bisshope þat bereþ croos, by þat he is holden
Thorw his provynce to passe and to his peple hym shewe.[29]

The episcopal imperative to "walk through one's province" is integral to the
ideal reflected in St. Thomas of Canterbury, and the repetition of the terms
"bishop(s)" and "cross" on either side underscores the pertinence of lines
570–71 to those culminating in 532.[30] The Kane-Donaldson and Schmidt
reconstruction does not remove the inconsequence, then: just moves it.

Given how important is this reconstruction for such foundational ideas
as the corruption of the C reviser's B manuscript and the relationship of the
two B-tradition manuscript families, it is startling to realize that the edi-
tors put forward no other supporting evidence. The rest of their discussion
focuses on the diagnosis of inconsequence, not the reconstruction itself, as in
the claim that in C "three revisions of detail relate to precisely the shortcom-
ings we sense in the passage."[31] In a footnote, Kane and Donaldson observe
that one C-version manuscript, Cotton Vespasian B XVI (M), transposes C
17.259–85β and 188–258, "that is to something like our rearrangement," be-
cause of sophistication or good correction,[32] but they misread the situation. It
is clear that the scribe responsible for the error simply copied the passage with
these lines as the second and third,

And perel for þe **prelates þat the pope makeþ**
Þat beren name of **neptalym of nynyve and of damasc**
(C 17.260–61, the revision of B 15.509–10)

in place of one that had these nearly identical words at the equivalent location,

So many **prestes to preche as þe pope makeþ**
Of nazareth of **nynyve of neptalym and of damasc** (C 17.188–89=B
15.493–94)

and eventually returned to correct his error, leading to the transposition of
259–85β and 188–258.[33] The W~M scribe of B made an almost identical error
concerning these titular bishops: having copied "That **bere** bisshopes **names**
of **bedlem** & babiloyne" (B 15.510), he resumed at the line just after "sovereyn-
liche to suche þat of **surrie bereth þe name**" (528), an error that Donaldson
cited as the best example of that scribe's proneness to eyeskip.[34]

None of these problems attends the proposal that the forty lines were originally intended for the 15.343α/344 juncture. Indeed, in this scenario *both* sites of the transition would be perfectly smooth. On the one side, the climax of a long consideration of the "Religiouse þat riche ben" would easily lead into lines 533–37:

> 340    Ryht so ʒe riche, ʒe robeth and fedeth
>
> Hem þat haen as ʒe haen; hem ʒe make at ese.
>
> Ac religious þat riche ben sholde rather feste beggares
>
> Than burgeys þat riche ben as þe boek techeth,
>
> *Quia sacrilegium est [etc.]*
>
> 533    Hit is reuthe to rede how riʒtwise men lyvede,
>
> How they deffouled here flesche, forsoke hir owne wille,
>
> Fer fro kuthe and fro kyn evele yclothed ʒeden,
>
> Baddeliche ybedded, no boek but conscience,
>
> Ne no rychesse but þe rode to rejoysen hem ynne.

The most felicitous effect of the juxtaposition would have been its dense focus upon the responsibilities of "the rich," similar to that upon the responsibilities of the episcopate at 523–32, 570–71.[35] Other motifs, too, resonate across this divide: before, the rich "robeth . . . hem þat haen as ʒe haen" (340–41); after, the righteous, by contrast, walk about "evele yclothed" (535). On this side, the rich religious should feed beggars "as þe boek techeth" (343); on that, the righteous have "no boek but conscience" (536). This whole contrast between the rich and poor began with the speaker's consideration of the examples found "in *legenda sanctorum*, þe lif of holy seyntes" (269); here Anima continues to expound that collection, remarking that it is piteous "to rede how riʒtwise men lyvede" (533). Likewise the other side of my reconstruction, especially if we accept Kane and Donaldson's emendation at 566 (*Charite*), based on C 17.231 (it seems clearly preferable to N²/W-M's non-alliterative "Good"), is marked by repetition of four charged terms across the juncture, with a perfect transitional term:

> 565    Yf possession be poysen and inparfit hem make
>
> **Charite** were to **deschargen** hem for holy churche sake,
>
> And **purge** hem of poysen ar more perel falle.
>
> Yf presthode were parfyt the peple sholde amende
>
> 569    That contraryen **cristes** lawe and **cristendoem** dispisen.

344    Forthy y consayle alle **cristene** to confourmen hem to **charite**,
       For **charite** withouten chalengynge **unchargeth** þe soule,
       And mony a prisoun fro **purgatorie** thorw hise preyeres
           delyvereth.

This reconstruction of Langland's intentions with regard to "533–69" is further supported by C's revisions at this site, where Langland newly invokes St. Lawrence, who "gaf goddes men goddes goodes and nat grete lordes" (C 17.67). Teresa Tavormina's claim that St. Lawrence "may well have been the last ecclesiastical administrator free of the 'poison of possession' " indicates his manifestation of the themes of our lines.[36] Langland continues by attempting to fix up the disjointedness of the received B passage. In B, immediately after counselling Christians to conform to Charity at my proposed juncture appears what Mary Carruthers calls "an odd *non sequitur*" in the shape of Langland's comparison of the false soul to the false coin from Luxemburg, the lushburg:[37]

Ac þer is a defaute in þe folk þat þe fayth kepeth,
Wherfore folk is þe febler and nat ferme of bileve.
As in lossheborwes is a luyþer alay, and ȝut loketh he lyk a sterlyng;
The marke of þat moneye is goed ac þe metal is feble.    (B 15.347–50)

Langland seems to have anticipated Carruthers. Perhaps as "a draft of a new introduction to the figure to replace its abrupt appearance in B 349" he turned from Lawrence back to this figure of the lushburg, so that Anima's original reference to bad money is no longer so abrupt:[38]

Me may now likene lettred men to a loscheborw oþer worse
And to a badde peny with a gode printe:
. . . . . . . . . . . . . . . . . . . . . . . . . . . . . . .
Thus ar ȝe luyþer ylikned to lossheborwe sterlynges.    (C 17.73–74, 83)

If the original plan had been activated, the image of the *crux denarii*, the cross on the coin, would have precipitated Anima's lushburg simile, which, like the *crux denarii*, is associated with "werre and wikkede werkes" (356): "And now is werre and wo, and hoso why asketh: / For coveytise after cros; þe croune stant in golde" (542–43). Here the simile would have served as a natural development of a figure that itself had appeared in an appropriate context only a few dozen lines earlier, rather than the 200-odd lines earlier as in Kane and Donaldson's text. The C revision, in other words, accomplishes what the "poison of possession" passage would have done had it remained in the location that first sparked it.

Might such indications be interpreted as evidence that the C reviser was here reconstructing an original no longer available to him—that is, that B 15.533–69 was part of the B version, but for some reason, such as the loose sheet's absence from his copy, unavailable to him as he revised? Not very easily, which I say not just because this proposal replicates the problems canvassed above regarding B scribes' inability or unwillingness to copy passages into their texts, but also, and more so, because it is clear that the lines were not absent at all. Else they could not turn up some 150 lines later in C 17. It makes much more sense to interpret the appearance here of the new Lawrence material instead as serving as a replacement for the "poison of possession" lines upon his decision to place them in that later location. Langland saw the 15.343α/344 juncture as the site of insertion of the Constantine lines when he initially sat down to revise his poem—but his plans changed, bringing about C 17 as we now have it, and enabling the production of B 15 as now printed in Kane and Donaldson. In sum, "B 15.533–69" was no such thing, with regard both to the line numbers and the version itself.

## RF/Cx Versus W-M/Nx

The manner of W-M's assimilation to Nx, then, is relatively straightforward. But what explains RF's lack of access to these lines? I will here argue that RF was produced after W-M, by which time the new Nx lines available to that scribe were no longer in Bx. In itself, this conclusion is not particularly noteworthy, at least if my interpretation of the LR rubric is accurate, for we already knew that Bx itself was the product of the C era, so its descendants must have been as well. But the evidence that leads to that conclusion is remarkable for uncovering yet another form of C > B contamination—a form that will play a central role in the argument of Chapter 4 below that the final two passus *in toto* came into B from C.

Some recent discussions of RF's lack of 15.533–69 have assumed its connection with the absence of 15.511–28 from W-M, but these strike me as forced and arbitrary.[39] For one, as noted above, these lines' absence from W-M is so easily explained as eyeskip from "That **bere** bisshopes **names** of **bedlem**

& babiloyne" (B 15.510) to "sovereynliche to suche þat of **surrie bereth þe name**" (528). While appeals to local scribal error run the risk of obscuring larger-scale patterns, there are no indications of any such pattern here. Indeed, if this instance is to be connected to any other manuscript, the obvious candidate is not RF but MS M of C, which as we have seen features a major dislocation brought about by eyeskip from prelates who bear names of Nephthali, Nineveh, and Damascus to priests who bear names of Nephthali, Nineveh, and Damascus. The two separate absences of 15.511–28 and 533–69 from the respective B traditions are no more obviously related than are those of, say, B 12.139–47α from RF and B 12.116–25α from W-M,[40] or of, over the space of 300-plus lines of C 11 alone, some forty-four omissions totalling over sixty-five lines by seventeen manuscripts or groups.[41] The proximity of any two errors does not indicate anything about the nature of either error.

Matters get more interesting at line 529, where W-M return, thus reading "That bere bisshopes names of bedlem & babiloyne / That huppe aboute in Ingelond to halewe men auters" (B 15.510, 529). As part of their separate cases that this W-M juncture is authorial, with the RF-only 511–28 representing a separate stage of composition, both Steven Justice and Sean Taylor have cited the syntax of RF's 528/29 juncture ("sovereynliche to suche þat of surrie bereth þe name, / And nat to huppe") as evidence that Langland revised this passage during the era of B-production. "What the Athlone edition (following the RF tradition) presents as its lines 526–30—which contrast today's shirking bishops with Thomas, the apostle and martyr—is a syntactical mess," claims Justice: "For the awkward 'And nauȝt to'—which lacks a first term for the implied grammatical parallelism—occurs just at the splice where RF includes lines that are not present in W," whereas the W-M version, by contrast, "supplements a grammatical parallelism with continuity of sense"; after noting the 533–69 phenomenon, he concludes simply that Langland wrote the passage twice, once with and once without St. Thomas.[42] How this supposed hash supports such a conclusion remains murky: the passage would have made perfect sense if Langland had retained "That" in both supposed versions. In any case, this syntax appears at least twice elsewhere in B: "That is þe professioun apertly þat apendeth to knyhtes, / *And nat to* fasten o friday in fyve score wynter" (B 1.100–101); "For when a werkeman haþ wrouht, þan may men se þe sothe, / What he were worthy for his werk and what he haþ deserved, / *And nat to* fonge before for drede of dessallouwynge" (B 14.137–39).

There is, however, an intriguing explanation for RF's syntax here. Over these four lines (15.529–32), RF (or (R ?= RF)) agrees with Cx against

Nx/W-M six times, beginning with this phrase *and nat to*.[43] This is the most concentrated instance of a larger pattern. Of the 131 readings where RF alone agrees with Cx from B 8/C 10 through B 18/C 20, $N^2$ agrees with W-M ninety-three times (71 percent), by contrast supporting the expected RF/Cx reading only twenty-eight times (21 percent; for the remaining ten $N^2$ is idiosyncratic).[44] This pattern extends from variants that in other contexts might appear scribal, as do hundreds of Langland's revisions, to occurrences for which coincident substitution is a very unsatisfactory explanation, such as RF's spurious derivation at 11.437, "no man loveth his felachipp," of C 13.243b, "uch man shoneth his companye," where $N^2$ and W-M have "for evry man him shon(y)eþ,"[45] and RF/Cx's "dobest" and "dronke aftur" for $N^2$/W-M's "dowel" and "toek þe coppe & dronke" (B 13.103–4/C 15.110–11).

The $N^2$/W-M agreements here, it seems clear, are peers to those sixty-four inherited from Bx, which simply had not been revised to their final C form by the time Nx was produced, and away from which RF would move at a subsequent stage of the poem's transmission. If these readings were instead the result of contamination in either direction, that is, W-M > Nx or Nx > W-M, it would be impossible to explain how it occurred so often where RF and Cx happen to agree. Likewise this can hardly be the result of RF > Cx contamination, unless the source of Bx's C-contamination, as discussed in the Preface, was a pre-archetypal text, since C was already circulating by the time RF's exemplar was produced. In any case, such an idea would not explain how these sites of contamination happened to correspond so overwhelmingly with those where Nx diverged from Cx. If, say, Nx did not support Cx for 5 or 10 percent of these readings, no one would be very surprised: but *80* percent?

My proposal, then, is that it is C that contaminated RF, after the earlier stage of C (i.e., Nx) had sent over sheets with entire passages to Bx as copied by W-M. Perhaps the RF scribe was being recompensed for his lack of the new materials to which his peer, the W-M scribe, had access. We know that between W-M's copying and the production of Cx these forty lines were supplemented by four new ones, together with nearly thirty other small revisions. It would be a reasonable, if not inevitable, supposition that the loose sheets that went from Nx to W-M were, if not Langland's only copies, very closely affiliated with him, so that they were recalled to enable the production of the final, C version of these passages.

Two other interesting and previously unrecognized phenomena bolster my proposal that C has contaminated RF on the level of individual line and lection, and are very difficult to account for otherwise. The first comprises

RF's substitution of spurious lines for $N^2$/W-M agreements, discussed in Chapter 2. At these junctures Bx seems to have been marked as superseded by passages not available to RF, prompting that scribe to exercise his imagination a bit. Yet such marking could hardly have occurred before the new material existed. So the RF scribe must have used Bx as exemplar after, not before, W-M, who was able to follow up on those marks' significance. Second is the pattern by which either of RF's constituent surviving manuscripts, R or F, agrees with $N^2$/W-M where the other agrees with C, which seems just too coincidental in the received account to be allowed to stand unchallenged now that its existence has come to light. Among the dozen or so instances between B 8/C 10 and B 18/C 20 are the attestation at B 8.6, by R alone, of C 10.6's "in þis world" for $N^2$/W-M/F "as I went," and in the passage discussed above, R's "amonges" at B 15.531 for $N^2$/W-M/F "in."[46] Kane and Donaldson explain W-M/F agreements in error as coincident variation, W-M/R ones either as correction in the immediate tradition of F or as coincident variation.[47] (R's reading at 8.6, strictly speaking, falls into neither of the editors' categories, since they judge it to be the sole erring B manuscript.) A simpler explanation is that the RF scribe recorded some or all of these new C readings as corrections to his manuscript, sometimes leading one of this exemplar's subsequent scribes (e.g., R) to attest the correction where the other (e.g., F) preferred the original.

The scars of C revision upon RF are suggested elsewhere as well, as in the RF-tradition's loss of some lines in a few instances where $N^2$ does not provide a check. Consider this Bx passage:

> Thenne y courbed on my knees and criede here of grace;
> And preyede here pitously to preye for my synnes;
> And also kenne me kyndly on crist to bileve,
> That y myhte worchen his wille þat wrouhte me to man.
> "Teche me to no tresor, but telle me this ilke,
> How y may save my soule, þat saynt art yholde" (B 1.79–84)

Kane and Donaldson quite reasonably explain RF's loss of line 82 as "omission of intervening syntactical unit through attraction of *kenne me . . . to* 81 to *Teche me to* 83."[48] But this is the only line of B 1.51–97 to be excised from C 1.47–93. It would now seem at least as likely that the line disappeared because it had been marked for cancellation in C, and thus in Bx as copied by RF as well. Likewise, of this passage,

Or who worse dede þan David þat Uryes deth conspired,
Or Poul þe apostel þat no pite hadde
Muche Cristene kynde to culle to dethe? (B 10.429–31)

the Athlone editors say that RF omitted the final line "through subconscious suggestion of the parallelism *Or . . . Dauid þat, Or Poul . . . þat*, that 430, like 429, was a completed statement."[49] Yet whatever physical aspect of Cx prompted all C manuscripts save one to run that line (11.267) together with its predecessor (i.e., "Poul þe apostel þat no pite hadde cristene peple to culle to dethe"), this physical phenomenon, if signaled in Bx as copied by RF, could easily have caused his trouble. Finally, this proposal accounts well for the large-scale loss of lines that afflicted both subarchetypal B scribes. A number of W-M's lost passages, in particular, can be mapped precisely upon the pattern of C's structural revision.[50]

The surviving evidence shows not only that Bx was a post-C production, but also that it bore heavy marks of the C text, far beyond the bizarre closing rubric about Dobest, in each of the two states in which it survives, W-M and RF. The "poison of possession" lines are the most spectacular instance we have encountered, yet it is the more mundane RF/Cx program that directs attentive readers to the most dramatic instance of C > B contamination, site of the erroneous "Dobest" rubric and of the heaviest concentration of RF/Cx agreements: that of the final two passus, which are at the core of the very identity of an integral "B version" c. 1378.

# Chapter 4

# The Ending, and End, of *Piers Plowman* B

Are passus 19 and 20 of *Piers Plowman* B the 1000-odd lines of Middle English poetry with the greatest impact upon our understandings of English culture c. 1380? Few competitors present themselves. These passus' sheer power has attracted much of the attention: Robert Frank heard "splendid Beethovian thunder" in passus 20, which features Will's waking encounter with Need and the apocalyptic final dream in which Elde and Antichrist ravage Holy Church.[1] The final few lines, in which Conscience announces that he "wol bicome a pilgrime, / And wenden as wyde as the world renneth / To seke Peres the Plouhman" and Will awakens one last time (B 20.380–82), have struck others as a perfect and even inevitable encapsulation of the irresolution of the poem: "What other ending can there be?" asked Skeat.[2] And on the basis of its role as the part of B most helpful in dating that version,[3] what the thunder said has generated arguments that B is "a London work and the culmination of Edwardian literature in the City,"[4] records Langland's investment in London city politics of the 1370s,[5] inspired Chaucer to write the *House of Fame*,[6] and incited the insurgents of 1381.[7] To a greater degree than even the "Donation of Constantine" passage, passus 19 and 20 have set the tone for modern criticism of *Piers Plowman*: without these episodes, the identity of "the B version," its place in history, and much of that history itself might look much different, if not disappear altogether.

This book has been cumulatively building the case that it may be time to prepare seriously for that prospect, and the introduction of the "Vita de Dobest" to the picture brings the situation to a head.[8] In the Preface we encountered the startling fact that this was site of the sole incontrovertible instance of C > Bx contamination apart from the program I have been discussing in this book. In this chapter I will argue that the rubric now extant in the LR manuscripts of B was the least of that movement: the 850 lines preceding it, too, were added to Bx from the C tradition. I begin by showing how, despite the silence about it, this possibility is in some ways preferable to the other explanations of the phenomenon of these two passus' nearly identical appearance in the B and C traditions. I then turn to the textual affiliations among the B- and C-tradition groups, showing that the paradigm currently in place relies upon extraordinarily, maybe impossibly, difficult assumptions about scribal behavior. These affiliations show that no single B 19–20 exists to begin with, since the two major B-tradition manuscript groups of that version differ as the result (so I will argue) of separate stages of authorial production. Finally, this chapter will suggest a narrative that would explain how this phenomenon came into being—one that, while complicated, is nevertheless simpler than are any alternatives currently available.

The primary result of this exercise will be so new that there might be little point in attaching the name "*Piers Plowman* B" to Langland's first revision of the poem at all. That identity is too bound up with the critical history of the poem at large. A longer version of the poem that lacks Meed's promise to pay for the windows in the friary, Wit's lines on sex, Anima's invective against the poison of possession, and especially these final visions of the building of Holy Church and its downfall at the hands of Sir *Penetrans Domos* occupies a different category: "ur-B" is useful for the moment, but perhaps at some point scholarship will find a productive way to discuss the stages of the poem without resorting to the letter scheme at all. In the pre-1390 longer version of the poem whose existence is here argued (which might never have circulated beyond Langland's inner circle), fraternal licentiousness is either the driving force behind, or the most obvious manifestation of, the downfall of the English church, and the final two passus of the C version are the site of Langland's later response to the Rising of 1381 and the condemnation of Wyclif in 1382. Holy Church Unity is within sight: but the wandering friars and "lollares" have succeeded in turning Christendom's eyes away from that goal, leading Conscience, in the closing lines *of C* rather than "of the poem" as we are accustomed to say, to begin the whole process anew.

## Opening Out the "Unrevised" Narrative

The problem of the nearly identical appearance of B 19–20 and C 21–22 is among the most widely recognized of *Piers Plowman*'s textual record. George Russell, architect of the modern approaches to the situation, proposed three possible explanations: either Langland was satisfied with these passus as they stood; or he did revise them, but they were absent from the copy of C being put together by Langland's literary executor or that version's first scribe, who made good the lack by recourse to a B manuscript; or—the option endorsed by both the Athlone editors and A. V. C. Schmidt—Langland died before he could complete his revisions.[9] Any account of Langland's career, or any attempt to edit, not to mention define, the longer versions of *Piers Plowman*, relies upon a decision about the status of C 21–22. To date, however, the phenomenon has in effect served as a touchstone for discussions of other problems: Russell and Kane find signs of extensive revision throughout the rest of C, on which basis they reject the explanation that Langland was satisfied with B 19–20; Ralph Hanna finds few signs of extensive revision throughout the rest of C, on which basis he endorses that same explanation.[10] In both cases what is really at stake are the critics' preconceptions about Langland's career rather than the phenomenon of "Dobest" itself.

Another problem with this approach is that it cannot be ruled out that C, like the BmBoCot manuscripts, is the result of a scribe's attempt to repair a defective manuscript by recourse to B. If true, this would undermine a major plank of the Athlone postulate of uncompleted revision.[11] On what grounds do Russell and Kane reject this possibility? Because "it fails to account for the other indications of uncompleted revision."[12] Yet even if we are to assume a connection between "Dobest" and another problem—and the grounds on which we are to do so remain unarticulated—how do we know it is this particular one? What, for instance, of the fact that their preferred explanation, that "incapacity or death put an end to the poet's revising,"[13] "fails to account for" the ample evidence that scribes turned to other exemplars to fix deficiencies?

The problem is compounded by the circumstance that deficiency is not the only, or even the primary, cause of scribes' seeking out exemplars from other traditions, and that, while the "other indications of uncompleted revision" would remain in *Piers Plowman* regardless of whether the last two passus evince them, there is another explanation of "Dobest" that has the potential to solve a longstanding problem of the Langlandian textual record. For, as we have seen, just when the C version materialized, readers began to become "jealous for the completeness of their copies."[14] This is surely the primary impulse behind the search for additional exemplars. Why, though, was this jealousy manifested only by recourse to the C and never to the B tradition in copies W, N, K, Z, and TH²Ch? It is certainly possible that chance alone accounts for this striking situation; but a more compelling explanation would be a circumstance that could apply to our problem as well: that it was

C 21–22 that entered the B manuscript tradition, which probably was not even available when these conflations were put together, rather than B being taken over to complete C. That these scribes' recourse only to C conclusions has always seemed to be a problem is itself the product of the assumption that B achieved early circulation.

This phenomenon aside, there are good reasons why the proposal that B 19–20 originated as C 21–22 should have been part of the conversation from the beginning. For one, the final trajectory of passus B 18 would work perfectly well as the final trajectory of the whole poem. "In a profound sense," Morton Bloomfield wrote in 1961, "the powerful scene of the Harrowing of Hell is the true end of the poem, of the quest for Christian perfection which this poem exemplifies"; after this, church bells awaken Will, who then urges Kit his wife and Calote his daughter to reverence the cross at mass on Easter morning.[15] "Had the B Version fallen silent after the Easter mass-bells, its likeness to the major Ricardian pieces would not have passed unremarked," comments A. V. C. Schmidt before rejecting my argument as "too startling" to be really probable: "Particularly noteworthy would have seemed its closeness to the most 'through-composed' of these poems, *Pearl*. For B 18.423–24 and *Pearl* 1208–10 both envisage the reception of Communion as the 'eschatological' symbolic act of *fratres habitantes in unum* (Ps. 132:1=B 18.423α), whereas now *Pearl* concludes virtually with an 'answer' to what is Langland's actual final passus."[16] And a moment's consideration of the late dates of all *Piers Plowman* manuscripts will dispense with the other seeming stumbling block to the proposal, as colorfully rendered by Robert Adams: "the conniving B scribes were so thorough in hiding this borrowing [by a B scribe of C's conclusion] that no surviving B witness provides a tangible clue of its having actually occurred, and nothing but the most erratic and highly contaminated C witness—MS N$^2$ (National Library of Wales MS 733B)—can be mustered into service to make the argument."[17] That it is the pattern of RF/C agreements, not the witness of N$^2$, that will generate my argument aside, such an objection undermines its own cause, since the conniving scribes were also so thorough in hiding their production of pre-1390 B copies ending with passus 20 that no surviving witness provides a tangible clue of their having actually existed. There are minimal signs of B's transmission before the C era whatever shape it took, so it is meaningless to cite the absence of one shape as evidence for the presence of the other.

At this point, regardless of which explanation of this most pressing of problems seems most compelling, we remain in the realm of speculation. For the standard narratives, in which the poet either died or was satisfied with

B 19–20, upon which so much scholarship about *Piers Plowman* and late medieval English culture has rested, are even more speculative than my own proposal, in that they fail to account for all the indications, throughout the manuscript record, of how scribes behaved in their efforts to record, and create, the collection of words we now call "*Piers Plowman* B."

## The Textual Assumptions of the B > C Narrative

To date all approaches to our problem have been the products of the regime delineated in Chapter 2, which assumes a transparent correlation between the "shapes" of the surviving traditions and the authorial "versions" with which those traditions originated. Here, they relied on the simple, and speculative, assumption that it was sufficient to determine the two archetypal texts, Bx and Cx, independently, and only then to compare the results—rather than the body of data on which they rely—with an eye towards determining the authorial text.[18] This is the effect of the assumption that the surviving shapes must be authorial, all indications to the contrary notwithstanding. The most influential such account is by the Athlone editors, in which the latest generation listed comprises the final, now-lost exclusive ancestors of all surviving manuscripts, which divide into two families each in both B and C. It can be represented by the stemma shown here.

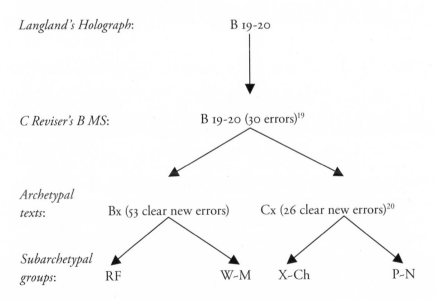

*Langland's Holograph*:    B 19-20

*C Reviser's B MS*:    B 19-20 (30 errors)[19]

*Archetypal texts*:    Bx (53 clear new errors)    Cx (26 clear new errors)[20]

*Subarchetypal groups*:    RF    W-M    X-Ch    P-N

But a comparison of *all* groups together in these passus, rather than only of the presumably distinct Bx and Cx groups, reveals a major difficulty that this paradigm cannot accommodate. In those places in the final two passus where it is straightforward to identify the readings of the four subarchetypal groups, there are about sixty-three readings (regardless of their status as authorial or erroneous, or "major" or "minor" if erroneous)[21] where RF and W-M agree together against Cx (i.e., X-Ch and P-N), as would be expected,[22] and 105—about one every eight or so lines—where RF or F(=?RF) instead agrees with Cx against W-M.[23] Now, if W-M, too, had a hundred of its own agreements with Cx against RF, this might not appear so dramatic, though we would have another remarkable problem to explain. Indeed we would expect roughly similar rates of agreement between each B family and Cx, given that neither subarchetypal scribe was particularly errant with regard to individual readings.[24] But the available figures show that W-M agrees with Cx against RF only about once every nineteen lines (column 2, row 3 in the chart), that is, about 230 percent less frequently than the situation we are considering (column 1, rows 2 and 3).[25]

| | *1. Number of RF/Cx (rows 1 and 3) or F/Cx (row 2) agreements vs. W-M* | *2. Number of W-M/Cx agreements vs. RF* |
| --- | --- | --- |
| **1. 18.1–410/20.1–453** **(c. 390 lines in common)** | 24 (1 / 16.3 lines) | 43 (1 / 9 lines) |
| **2. 19/21.1–20/22.26** **(c. 506 lines in common;** **R deficient)** | 58 (1 / 8.7 lines) | Unknowable |
| **3. 20/22.27–386** **(c. 360 lines in common)** | 47 (1 / 7.7 lines) | 19 (1 / 19 lines) |

If not for the fact that RF clearly shares a substantial number of errors with W-M, from this showing it might even appear that it is Cx, rather than the other B subarchetype, that pairs with RF as a witness to a common exemplar.[26]

The sharp break that separates the last two passus from the previous one is particularly striking here. In a situation of randomizing scribal behavior, we would find relatively stable rates of RF/Cx and W-M/Cx agreement throughout the poem: what happens in the last two passus would continue what happened before. Unfortunately, both because B and C are much further apart earlier in the B-continuation than they are in these two passus and because there is no place where we can be confident that differences between W-M and RF are the products of such randomness, there is little basis for a thorough comparison. Even with such caveats in mind, however, the chart above shows how startling are the differences between B 19–20/C 21–22 and B 18/C 20, that passus where the two versions are closer to each other than anywhere except these final two passus: the density of RF/Cx agreements doubles between 18/20 (one per sixteen lines) and "Dobest" (one per eight lines), while that of W-M/Cx is more than halved, from one every nine lines—an unusually dense figure itself[27]—to one per nineteen.[28]

This assimilation of RF to Cx in "Dobest" makes it just about impossible to construct a narrative of the production of these three copies, W-M, RF, and Cx, that will fit the standard paradigm. If RF and W-M are witnesses to an identical Bx, then wherever they conflict only one of them (at most) can have the correct reading. In our scenario, though, however we distribute the errors, enormous difficulties arise. In Schmidt's approach, any agreement between either RF or W-M with Cx against the other group is, as a rule, evidence against the odd reading out: of the 105 RF/Cx agreements in B 19–20 he deems all but six authorial.[29] The logic is straightforward. Yet its result is the utter collapse of W-M's facility as a copyist upon reaching this material: in passus 18 he had strayed from the correct RF/Cx reading only once every sixteen lines (column 1, row 1), but in 19–20 he suddenly descended to a rate of once every nine lines (i.e., 99 errors in c. 866 lines). And he is alone in this sudden incompetence, for in both the Schmidt and Athlone texts of passus 20, RF conflicts with correct W-M/Cx only once every *nineteen* lines (column 2, row 3; as noted above, though, it does seem that RF himself was quite errant in passus 18). Those who maintain this approach need to explain what characteristic of 19–20 prompts this collapse. It would be difficult to do so without granting the premise of my argument: that the final two passus are textually distinct from the rest of the B version.

The Athlone text, which distributes a substantial group of those errors to RF/Cx, exemplifies the alternative approach. This one makes the W-M scribe look a bit more competent, but necessitates the allowance that RF and Cx, or F and Cx, arrived independently at the identical error (unless that reading came into W-M via either correction against a pre-archetypal copy or felicitous conjecture). It thus does not faze Russell and Kane to find a number of agreements in error between F and Cx in B 19/C 21. "Two considerations made it possible to edit here," they comment: "an agreement of R and F in the absence of one of them was an unassessable possibility; meanwhile the variants in which F and the C tradition agreed were of a character likely to have occurred coincidentally."[30] Manuscript F's frequent pairing in erroneous readings with a number of other W-M manuscripts makes this particularly easy to grant.[31]

But neither coincident variation nor F's promiscuity can account for the dense cluster of F/Cx agreements in error Russell and Kane find over the 500 or so lines absent from R in this portion of the poem: about twenty-eight, just under half of their total number of agreements.[32] This rate of about one shared error every eighteen lines, if maintained over the course of the poem's roughly 7120 total lines, would add up to nearly 400 errors in common, a rate matched only by the most pervasively attested genetic groups, such as RF itself.[33] Moreover, Russell and Kane must surmise that MS F behaves in an unprecedented manner only where its sibling R happens to be deficient, yet is very disciplined (at least where C is concerned) everywhere else. In the surrounding passus where R is extant the Athlone editors identify only about twelve or so RF/Cx errors in 750 lines—a rate of one per sixty-three lines, three and a half times less dense than where R is deficient[34]—and no F/Cx errors where R has the correct reading.

This attempt to salvage the W-M scribe's reputation has not helped matters anyway. The attribution of twenty-eight errors to F/Cx has put those texts in an impossible situation, yet done almost nothing for W-M, whose seventy-odd remaining errors would still average out to one every twelve or so lines. The W-M scribe could appear competent in these passus only if the amount of coincident substitution attributed to RF and Cx were loaded up to such great proportions as to create an even bigger problem. There is no middle ground: an explanation of the B 19–20/C 21–22 problem must be somewhere other than in the standard narrative, which confers, without explanation, an extraordinary distinctiveness upon that portion of the poem Langland's readers began calling "Dobest."[35]

## Episode IV: A New Hope

The sole remaining viable explanation, I will now argue, is the reverse: that the RF scribe was influenced in some manner by C readings. It follows as well that B 19–20 in both extant forms, RF and W-M, came into the B tradition from C, with the differences between the two subarchetypal texts constituting evidence of Langlandian tinkering with this new material in the time between its sojourns with these two scribes. This is, I acknowledge, a difficult narrative, but not nearly as difficult as the standard approach. And it is bolstered by the existence of the pattern of $N^2$/W-M agreements discussed in Chapters 2 and 3, which can be explained only by positing just such C impact upon the two groups of the B tradition. It will be helpful to recapitulate the workings of the phenomenon, treated above in somewhat more piecemeal fashion. $N^2$—the sole survivor of the line of transmission inaugurated by the lost ancestor Nx—agrees with one or both of the B-tradition groups for a total of 251 readings, in five categories: (1) sixty-four with Bx; (2) ninety-three with W-M where RF = Cx, creating a chiasmus in which a supposed C manuscript agrees with half of B where the other half of B agrees with the rest of C; (3) five with W-M where RF is wild or deficient, readings that could support either of the previous two categories; (4) four with RF alone, of which only one very minor instance occurs where W-M is attested (*om.* "þat" at B 18.69/C 20.71); these could either be coincidental, as the one cited surely is, or provide support for item 1; and (5) eighty-five with W-M alone, among eighty-one lines where RF either has nothing or substitutes spurious material, including the materials from passus 3, 8, 9, 12, 15, and 16 discussed in Chapters 2 and 3.

This remarkable pattern of Nx/W-M agreements, I have argued above, is most efficiently explained as the result of three stages of transmission among these copies. First is that in which the sixty-four readings of item 1 had not yet been revised from Bx to Nx, which represents an early stage of the C version. The next two stages easily accommodate the problem of "Dobest," which, we need to remember, would otherwise be insurmountable. Most of the eighty-five agreements of item 5 came about when loose sheets of revision material went from Nx to Bx as copied by the scribe of the W-M ancestor. These passages, though, had been recalled, perhaps even for final revisions by the author, by the time RF sat down with Bx. That the major such instance, the "poison of possession" passage (K-D 15.533–69), is misplaced in W-M and absent from RF had already led a number of critics to postulate that it was on a loose sheet;[36] Nx's then-unknown behavior only cements the case. In our scenario, "Dobest" was among these passages, but either was not recalled with the other material, or was recalled but subsequently returned to Bx, with new "C" readings now recorded as corrections, before RF made his copy. And we have seen five or six reasons why the converse of my proposal, which would have it that this material went from W-M to Nx rather than the other way around, is untenable. At this stage, then, my proposal that C 21–22 turned into B 19–20 should appear at least as likely an explanation as would the notion that "Dobest" was integral to the B text.

Item 2, first discussed in Chapter 3's section on the B 15.528/29 juncture, accommodates the second part of the problem at issue here: the cluster of RF/ Cx agreements. By the time RF set to copying Bx, although he lacked the Nx passages to which W-M had access (e.g., that on the Donation of Constantine), he was in turn provided with subsequent revisions of the Nx "Dobest" into the form we would now call "C." This postulate would explain not only the cluster of RF/Cx agreements, but also the dozen or so instances where either MS R or F agrees with Nx/W-M against the other and Cx. Scribes R and $\alpha^1$ (i.e., that of F's exemplar) were here responding differently to corrections (i.e., new C readings) recorded in their exemplar, RF. At the ninety-odd readings where RF agrees with Cx against Nx/W-M, the W-M subarchetypal family in fact attests what we might for now call the "ur-B" *Piers Plowman*. So, too, at the hundred or so places in "Dobest" where RF agrees with Cx against W-M, the latter attests the "ur-C" text (=Nx), as it were, with RF attesting the revised, "C" version of the reading.

This proposal accords with the presence of affiliations that look very much like those that enabled the production of this narrative in the first place. For where F and Cx pair in 19/21, Nx continues to pair steadily, if not as consistently as before, with W-M against F/Cx: while still clearly a witness to C here,[37] Nx agrees about seventeen times each with W-M and F/Cx.[38] Nx's affiliations also suggest that the revisions to "Dobest" left Langland's desk at two different stages: the first movement is visible where Nx (Cx's ancestor) has received the RF/Cx reading; the second, where Nx still agrees with W-M, which are readings that together with the first group were sent to Cx and then RF. While it cannot be known whether the last two passus were recalled from and then returned to Bx, it is clear that when RF copied them their text had been altered. Here, then, is a visual representation of this narrative—in effect, a new stemma to replace the one above (see next page).

Why does the first line of this new stemma say "C 21–22" rather than "B 19–20"? On its own, this account of the various affiliations of N[2] and RF does not necessitate the conclusion that "Dobest" was not integral to the B version. Cx and RF's ninety-odd agreements against N[2] and W-M through passus 18/20, after all, are of matter integral to the "ur-B" *Piers Plowman* that remained unrevised in the early stages of C's life; and the evidence that sheets of material went from Nx to W-M merely accommodates the idea that "Dobest" was included among this matter. The first line says "C 21–22," then,

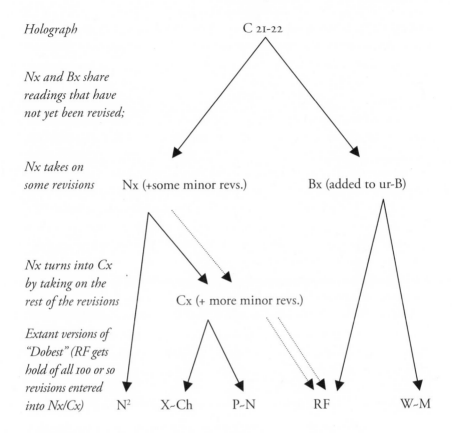

*Holograph*

C 21-22

*Nx and Bx share*
*readings that have*
*not yet been revised;*

*Nx takes on*
*some revisions*   Nx (+some minor revs.)   Bx (added to ur-B)

*Nx turns into Cx*
*by taking on the*
*rest of the revisions*   Cx (+ more minor revs.)

*Extant versions of*
*"Dobest" (RF gets*
*hold of all 100 or so*
*revisions entered*
*into Nx/Cx)*   N² X-Ch   P-N   RF   W-M

because of two other circumstances, each of which on its own would render my proposal the more likely, and which together present what I take to be insurmountable difficulties to any account other than this one. First is a phenomenon that keeps arising in this chapter: the distinctiveness of the last two passus, manifested in the density of the RF/Cx cluster of agreements, which occur about the same number of times, c. 100, over their 850-odd lines as over the preceding *4000* lines. That the W-M and C versions of these two passus were already much closer in character than is a great proportion of the earlier material only underscores the prominence of this characteristic: for it is sites of variation, not sameness, that attract "correction" and "contamination." If "Dobest" was a late entry to the B tradition, this distinctiveness is unsurprising; if not, this major problem remains in need of explication.

Second is the feature of "Dobest" upon which everyone to date has focused, and which Russell and Kane take as evidence "that the poet in his revising did not even look over these two passus": the absence of any substantive deletions, additions, or even, and most tellingly, corrections of unalliterative lines.[39] It is difficult to fathom why, as long as a decade after first composing these passus, Langland would have made so many fussy minor changes, yet no major ones. The nineteen unalliterative lines in both B and C versions of *Piers Plowman* would thus seem to be evidence not of a failure to revise, but rather of a separate phenomenon that Russell and Kane identify as occurring throughout the C version, likewise in support of their postulate of uncompleted revision: "a purpose not yet fully realized, as if there had been a postponement of attention to poetic form, whether through preoccupation with particular meaning, or a distracting sense of urgency about larger plans and changes."[40] The differences between W~M and RF/Cx, that is, are suggestive of the sorts of fits and starts that attend the *early* stages of composition, the sorts one might make on a quick second glance at the draft of a major project, putting off for the time being the intense labor of correction.

## The Structure of *Piers Plowman* in a Post-1381 World

It would be understandable if my argument that "B.19–20" entered that tradition from C were to prompt variations on the theme, "but this cannot be: it is not the Langland we know." Thus Schmidt, having noted the parallels between *Pearl* and a postulated B version lacking passus 19 and 20, rejects the possibility by asserting that "the building of Unity and the immediate attack on it would seem (to most readers) thematically indispensable if B's conception of Grace's activity in time is to be completed and 'salvation history' shown as continuing into the present."[41] This is circular, though. If history had played out differently and someone were arguing that "Dobest" was in fact integral to a poem long believed to have ended with passus 18, well-rehearsed arguments about the structural integrity of the shorter received poem would no doubt be marshalled as counter-evidence.[42] "Indispensable" is another term for "assumed to be integral," an attitude that does not constitute an argument against all the textual indicators that these passus were *not* integral to B.

In any case the reconciliation of my findings with earlier assumptions is not so difficult as might first appear: Langland might well have agreed with Schmidt, explaining the addition of these two passus, and perhaps even his holding back on the release of B in the first place. It needed a proper conclusion. The fact that, as Stephen Barney puts it, "the last two passus in some ways recapitulate earlier segments of the poem, particularly the second vision, the half-acre scene,"[43] might be said to make much more sense as the product of a post-1381 world than the one to which it has always been assigned. In 1929 Henry Wells identified deliberate parallels between "The Plowman's Pardon" of B passus 7 ("The plow of the honest laborer; hope for salvation of the individual; satire on indulgences; the active life") and the *Vita de Dobest* ("The mystic plow with which Christ cultivates souls; despair for the spiritual welfare of Christian Society (*Unitas*); satire on indulgences; the active life (Part II): Christ as Preacher; the cure of souls").[44] An obvious, if not exclusive, cause for this is found in an item central to Chapter 1: "Johon Schep . . . biddeþ Peres Plouȝman go to his werk, and chastise wel Hobbe þe Robbere": the "plowman's pardon" is the one episode that everyone will agree John Ball knew (if he knew any at all), and "Dobest" was where Langland sought to reclaim his poem, replacing "the plow of the honest laborer" with "the mystic plow." Future research into Langland's response to the Rising of 1381 might benefit from placing these two passus at the center.[45]

Any comprehensive narrative of the production of "Dobest"—which is to say, of the production of the longer versions of *Piers Plowman*, and of the histories with which this poem engages and that it in large part constitutes—must account for all of the textual problems addressed in this chapter. The renovation of some interpretations honed over generations of scholarship, like that put forth by Wells, shows that, while plenty of work might lie ahead of us, it will build upon and recalibrate, rather than replace, the established field of Langland studies. Any such efforts will need to engage with the evidence on which I am claiming that "B 19–20" began life as C 21–22—or, to put it another way, that "*Piers Plowman* B" began life in a form nearly unrecognizable in modern discussions of that entity, and remained in that state, perhaps unnoticed by anyone, until the C version finally brought the great work into the public eye and recast "B" in its mold.

# Lollars, Friars, and *Fyndynges*: C Passus 9 and the Creation of *Piers Plowman*

*Piers Plowman* B was a much different poem, so I have argued, from the entity Skeat and his successors constructed and that has been studied ever since. This stage of the poem, which took shape in the late 1370s, lacked a series of passages totalling about eighty lines from passus 3, 8, 9, 12, 15, and 16; lacked the final two passus altogether; and had not yet taken on those hundred or so RF/Cx readings that conflict with W-M/N². But we can cast this in positive terms as well: over the course of the 1380s Langland put together a program that associates friars, illicit sexuality, and the question of *fyndynge* (that is, livelihood or endowment) in a series of passages first inscribed on loose sheets that could be read or copied independently and then incorporated into the C and W-M shapes of the poem. Langland seems to have produced all this material in a remarkable burst of creativity. For instance, Sir *Penetrans Domos*'s gift to Contrition, of

> a plastre
> Of "a pryve payement and y shal preye for 30w
> And for hem þat 3e aren holde to al my lyf tyme
> And make of 30w *memoria* in masse and in matynes
> As freres of oure fraternite for a litel sulver" (C 22.363–67)

revisits the friars' election of Meed as sister of the friary in return for her donation of the window in passus 3.[1] While Meed wants the friars to overlook the sin of lechery, Sir *Penetrans Domos* incarnates that sin: Peace says that he once "salved so oure wymmen til some were with childe" (347). Conscience concludes the poem by expressing the wish "þat freres hadde a fyndynge þat for nede flateren" (383)—in which case no more need to hop about in England rather than attending to their flocks, or to creep in among curates, or to woo Meed, or to penetrate into houses.[2]

That the bulk of the passages I have been discussing solely with regard to their textual affiliations are so united thematically constitutes, it seems to me, final, and as it were external, support for my argument that they went from Nx to Bx. It also sheds light on another very similar phenomenon first recognized by Wendy Scase twenty years ago, when she pointed out that in the appearance of a variant tradition of the C 9 materials on "lollares" and bad bishops in the Ilchester Prologue and the conflated Huntington 114's passus 6 "we have, quite exceptionally, internal evidence which corroborates the early, separate circulation, and subsequent rethinking, and revision, suggested by the textual evidence."[3] This is precisely what I am arguing we have in the $N^2$/ W-M pattern, and in the final two passus as well. Russell and Kane's remark that the C material shared by Ht and $N^2$ most likely had a common source, together with the fact that this material shares so many thematic concerns, suggests the probability that all of this matter originated together and entered circulation in similar form.[4] Perhaps the C passus 9 lines got separated from the "Poison of Possession" lines and their peers, the former making their way into the hands of Scribe D, the latter into those of his London neighbor, the W-M scribe.

In this C passus 9 material, which I quote below as it appears in the Ilchester Prologue, Langland expounds the damaging effects of false absolution, particularly in the episcopate. Instead of being good shepherds by administering tar (that is, "toughness in the confessional, refusing to absolve without restitution and penance that hurts") to their sheep's scabs, bishops in effect grant *supersedeas*, writs of stay:[5]

> For many waker wolves walken in þe feeldes;
> And þe barkers arn blynde þat bringe forþ þe lambes:
> *Dispergentur oves*, þe dogge dar not berk.
> Þe tarre is so untydy þat to þe scheep longes;
> Þair salve is supersedeas in somonours [boxes];
> Þe scheep ere all shabbed; þe wolf bischi[t wolle]:
> *Sub molli pastore [lupus lanam cacat] et grex [&c.]* (C 9.260–65α)

Langland was concerned with friar-bishops who have become wolves rather than serving as good shepherds as well when composing "Dobest": as Traugott

Lawler says, "all the business about 'tar' or 'salve' connects this passage with the last scene of the poem. I feel certain that when Langland added this stunning passage on corrupt bishops to the C version, he had that last scene in mind, and was preparing his readers for it."[6]

Lawler imagines Langland as thinking of the five uses of *salve* over the final eighty lines, such as

> Consience calde a leche þat couthe wel shryve:
> "Go salve tho þat syke ben and thorw synne ywounded."
> Shrift schupte scharp salve and made men do penaunse
> For here mysfetes that thei wrouht hadde
> And þat Peres pardon were ypayd, *redde quod debes.*
> Somme liked nat this leche and letteres they sente
> Yf eny surgien were in þe sege that softur couthe plastre. (C 22.304–10)

The new surgeon, Sir *Penetrans Domos*, administers the plaster "of payment" cited above. He is of course a friar: one of the "[lollares,] lacchedrawers, lewed hermites" who, says the new passus 9 matter, were once workers but abandoned that life when they "aspie[d] / How freres and oþer faytours hadden fatte chekes" (C 9.193, 208–9). Langland contrasts these *lollares* with the holy hermits of yore "þat woned in þe woode wiþ wolves and leons," to whom "briddes broghte bred þat þai by [lyv]ed" (197, 201).

Before I noticed the thematic closeness of all these passages, I had already speculated that a thirteen-line passage stuck in B passus 15 came into Bx together with the final two passus. That its theme, too, is the *fyndynge* of the righteous religious, and that Langland's revisions of this passage in C 17 are so closely linked with the new materials in C 9, suggest that it might merit inclusion in our analysis of this episode of his career. As received, in these lines Anima discusses the contemporary followers of the apostles:

> Ankerus and eremytes and monkes and freres
> Peeren to apostles thorw hire parfit lyvynge.
> Wolde nevere þe faythfull fader þat these mynistres sholde
> Of tyrauntes þat teneth trewe men taken eny almesse,
> But doen as Antony dede, Dominik and Fraunceys,
> Bothe Benet and Bernard, þe whiche hem furste tauhte
> To lyve by litel and in lowe houses by lele mennes almesse.
> Grace sholde growe and be grene thorw hir goode lyvynge,

And folke sholden fynde, þat ben in diverse seknesse,
The bettere for hir biddynges in body and in soule.
Hir preyeres and hir penaunces to pees sholde brynge
Alle þat ben at debat and bedemen were trewe:
*Petite & accipietis &c.* (B 15.417–28α)

The two characteristics that lead me to suspect that this was not integral to B are that, like the Donation of Constantine passage, in received B this interrupts a developing discourse about evangelism, not alms—before, Anima bewails Mohammed's success in bringing men and women into misbelief; after, he calls upon church leaders to turn the world to the one true faith—and that half of these lines end up revised in C passus 17, suggesting its character as draft material.[7] Its final form in C remarks with regard to the hermit Paul that "foules hym fedde" (17.15), showing how close was Langland's thinking in composing these thirteen lines, the material on lollares and hermits in C passus 9, and the opening of C 17.[8] Perhaps this does not constitute proof that the lines on anchorites were part of this program, but neither is there any proof that they were integral to B. If my hunch is right, then we need to look beyond the final two passus and their concluding rubric when considering the extent of C's impact on Bx, even where both B families attest the passage.

All these cross-references among passus 9, 17, and 22 of C and 15 of B emphasize that "Dobest" is the site of Langland's most extensive dramatization of the appearance of "lollards" on the English landscape. For as the C passus 9 passage indicates, and as Andrew Cole has argued meticulously, Langland's effort here "is to show that 'lollardy' is a construct—an utterance with a politically hostile valence that must be carefully weighed and, if need be, redirected against persons who are thought to be materially or economically unproductive, wasters and friars."[9] The bishops who need to protect their flocks from wolves in sheep's clothing do indeed need to remain alert for the presence of "lollares," but that does not necessarily mean "Wycliffites," as Archbishop Courtenay's 1382 injunction would have it.[10] In all the materials that went from Nx to W-M, as well as in the independently circulating C 9 meditation upon "lollares" and unwatchful bishops, Langland is responding to, or, as is perhaps a more accurate description, creating the world in which "lollardy" would become, despite his own alternative vision, the lightning-rod for accusations of heresy and deviance.

If my arguments are valid, they uncover some features of Langland's process of composition in specific ways previously unknowable. But the authorial end of the production/consumption spectrum on which, as Paul Eggert urges, we need to locate the "work" is not the only one that now looks different.[11] So does the consumption end, which, as we have seen, is not far removed at all from Langland's earliest production of C in particular. The example of Chaucer might illuminate the situation. In the wake of the success of Chaucer's longer poems, so it seems, lesser-known poems such as the *Book of the Duchess* were revived by enterprising literary agents and anthologized with other "minor" Chaucerian and Lydgatean poetry so as to meet market demand. John Stanley, for whom Oxford, Bodleian MS Fairfax 16 was produced, "did not choose single works or authors but booklets containing authors or works possibly in already existing saleable copy, or ready to be copied up from resident display booklets," observes John Norton-Smith. The copy Stanley procured turned out to be "the most beautifully produced and textually responsible example of the fifteenth century's desire to collect Chaucer and his poetic disciples," a desire owing to the high reputation of the *Troilus* and *Canterbury Tales* in particular.[12]

Did the converse of this happen with regard to Langland's work? Were the A version of *Piers Plowman* and a disparate group of sheets and booklets of timely poetry on the friars and ecclesiastical ethics the foundation of Langland's reputation, leading to the subsequent release of the two longer versions, both of which accommodated some of that matter regardless of its appropriateness to the dramatic context? If so, the differences from the Chaucer situation should not surprise us, especially given that *Piers Plowman* is long, often rambling, and accommodating of various genres and topics—in sum, quite different from the *Book of the Duchess* and its companions. A closer parallel would be the insertion of the *Canon's Yeoman's Tale* and even the *Tale of Gamelyn* into the similarly capacious Canterbury collection. But the biggest difference lies in Langland's consistent use of the long-line alliterative form, which allows any and all of his known verse to fall under the banner of "*Piers Plowman*," whereas there would be little room for Chaucer's minor verse in the *Canterbury Tales*.

Chaucer left behind discrete and identifiable poems; Langland left behind—how else to put it?—*Piers Plowman*, a work not able to be attributed to him alone, but rather comprising innumerable acts of production and intervention from the 1360s to today. While we lose something in the recognition that "*Piers Plowman* B" is a modern amalgam of three traditions brought together in the 1390s rather than a unified and complete poem available for quoting by c. 1379, then, we are abundantly recompensed by the opportunity to witness the formation, not only by Langland himself but also by the jealous scribes of his poetry, of the radically new English cultural landscape of the final decade of Richard II's reign and Chaucer's life, whose contours have only begun to be mapped by readers of *Piers Plowman* in its longer shapes and versions. In inviting jealous scribes, early conflators, George Kane, rebels, Chaucer, and everyone else who encountered *Piers Plowman* to participate in the ongoing creation of that work, Langland in effect hid himself from history, but gifted to it the most magnificent of poems, one still in the process of becoming, whether or not Conscience is still seeking Piers the Plowman.

# *Notes*

PREFACE

1. For an overview of critics' dating of B to these years, see Ralph Hanna, *William Langland* (Aldershot: Variorum, 1993), 12–14.

2. RF has long been known as a distinct family and called thus; see, e.g., E. Talbot Donaldson, "MSS R and F in the B-Tradition of *Piers Plowman*," *Transactions of the Connecticut Academy of Arts and Sciences* 39 (1955): 179–212. I use it in preference to A. V. C. Schmidt's α solely because of its prominence in such discussions throughout the history of the poem's textual study. See Schmidt, *"Piers Plowman": A Parallel-Text Edition of the A, B, C and Z Versions*, vol. 2, *Introduction, Textual Notes, Commentary, Bibliography and Indexical Glossary* (Kalamazoo, Mich.: Medieval Institute Publications, 2008), 142–47, and George Kane and E. Talbot Donaldson, eds., *"Piers Plowman": The B Version*, rev. ed. (Berkeley: University of California Press; London: Athlone, 1988), 25–28 on this family. See Schmidt, 126–42, and Kane and Donaldson, 54–59, on the WHmCrGYOC²CBLM family (which Schmidt calls β). George Russell and George Kane use W-M as an abbreviation for this group in their *"Piers Plowman": The C Version* (Berkeley: University of California Press; London: Athlone, 1997), 123, and I follow suit for the sake of consistency.

3. J. A. Burrow, "The Structure of *Piers Plowman* B XV–XX: Evidence from the Rubrics," *Medium Ævum* 77 (2008): 307.

4. Robert Adams, "The Reliability of the Rubrics in the B-Text of *Piers Plowman*," *Medium Ævum* 54 (1985): 214n11.

5. C. David Benson and Lynne Blanchfield, *The Manuscripts of "Piers Plowman": The B-Version* (Cambridge: D.S. Brewer, 1997), 191.

6. Robert Adams, "Evidence for the Stemma of the *Piers Plowman* B Manuscripts," *Studies in Bibliography* 53 (2000): 175.

7. Robert Adams, "Langland's *Ordinatio*: The *Visio* and the *Vita* Once More," *YLS* 8 (1994): 58.

8. Burrow, "Structure," attempts to combine literary with textual evidence, but in my opinion only the former is valid, and even that does not at all necessarily suggest that the rubrics were authorial. He points out that critics long ago recognized important transitional points in both passus 15 and 19, which would seem to suggest the validity of MSS W and L's "split rubrics" for these two passus (respectively, explicit Dowel, incipit Dobet; explicit Dobet, incipit Dobest). Since the LW rubrics most likely originate in Bx, they are

probably authorial. Regardless of the inevitable conclusion that at least one rubric from Bx originated in C, which Burrow does not mention, we might note that a good early reader could easily have come upon the scheme he identifies. Adams's "Reliability of the Rubrics" reads like a riposte to Burrow before the fact. Ralph Hanna, like Burrow, assumes that Bx's rubrics must be authorial, but his logic is difficult to follow; see "George Kane and the Invention of Textual Thought: Retrospect and Prospect," *YLS* 24 (2010). Lawrence Clopper, who takes the rubrication scheme in general to be authorial, nevertheless believes that the B rubrics are erroneous and thus scribal: "Langland's Markings for the Structure of *Piers Plowman*," *Modern Philology* 85 (1988): 245–55.

9. See Kane and Donaldson, *The B Version*, 70–97 on the archetypal B manuscript, 98–127 on the C reviser's B manuscript, and 165–73 on F.

10. George Kane, ed., *"Piers Plowman": The A Version*, rev. ed. (Berkeley: University of California Press; London: Athlone, 1988), 38.

11. Schmidt remarks that MS R "is present at the end to supply its own distinctive reading," referring to Adams's contention that this came into R from C (*Parallel-Text*, 940, 942n3), but does not reveal the rubric's wording. Nor does he note MS L's guide for the rubricator. Kane's descriptions of A-version manuscripts cite their rubrics, but that policy is abandoned in the B and C editions (see Adams, "Reliability," 214n9).

12. E. Talbot Donaldson, *"Piers Plowman": The C-Text and Its Poet* (New Haven, Conn.: Yale University Press, 1949; rpt. London: Frank Cass, 1966), 28. Russell and Kane say the C version originated as a marked-up B manuscript with "larger insertions of new material on slips of membrane, interleaved or stitched to leaves at their point of insertion," and "well more than a dozen separate single leaves or bifolia of new material, interleaved or loose" (*The C Version*, 89). Schmidt, by contrast, prefers the idea that Langland "planned his structural and verbal alterations in rough working papers and then re-drafted the new text one or more times as he progressed towards a fair copy" or wrote out the copy fresh, an amanuensis making a fair copy (*Parallel-Text*, 62), but I find the Athlone editors' approach much more convincing.

13. In all quotations of medieval materials, whether from editions or manuscript sources, I have followed most of H. A. Kelly's "rules for re-editing medieval texts," especially distinguishing between the two forms of the letters *u/v* and *i/j* and inserting modern capitalization or removing medieval capitalization (though otherwise I adopt the Athlone punctuation). See "Uniformity and Sense in Editing and Citing Medieval Texts," *Medieval Academy News* 148 (Spring 2004): 8–9. I do not, though, replace yogh and thorn with modern equivalents as Kelly suggests, since unlike the cases of *u/v* and *i/j* there is no risk of confusing readers, and it seems likely that these symbols are important in dialectal analysis, as suggested by Michael Benskin, "The Letters <þ> and <y> in Later Middle English, and Some Related Matters," *Journal of the Society of Archivists* 7 (1982): 13–30, and Gene Lyman, "Scribal Grapholects: Allographic Substitutions and the Textual Transmission of *Piers Plowman* B," presented at the Fourth International *Piers Plowman* Conference, University of Pennsylvania, 17 May 2007. The reproduction of editorial brackets is common in Langland criticism, but to my knowledge unprecedented elsewhere in English studies. While Schmidt says that the "irresponsible practice" of

"spiriting away the multitudinous brackets around their emendations, as is regularly done by critics who do not fully grasp their implications" is the "unhappy effect of [the Athlone edition's] use as the normal citation-text" (*Parallel-Text*, 60, cf. 36), this seems to me to confuse the issue. Brackets are intended only to signal departure from copy-text (and even then, do not appear where copy-text readings are omitted) and not to represent readers' desire to signal the texts's "editedness," so any irresponsibility inheres not in spiriting them away, but in assuming that real engagement with the edition inheres in one's response to them. The Athlone editors continually remark, after all, that non-bracketed readings are no less "edited" than bracketed ones. Kane, *The A Version*, 167; Russell and Kane, *The C Version*, 137.

14. They remark: "10.62 *wide*] D; *wilde* arch. This line was rejected by the B editors as intrusive from C (8.63); in the archetypal B form, to go by HmCr's variant, the text read *wyde*. Substitution of *wilde* for *wide*, predictable in this expression, occurred again in the archetype at 19.54 where, however, it is Ch that was corrected" (Russell and Kane, *The C Version*, 165). In the B edition Kane and Donaldson had merely diagnosed received B 8.62–63 as omission of the authorial reading by eyeskip, resulting in "one line with later padding," but they indicate neither just how late the padding occurred nor its source (*The B Version*, 99).

15. *Wilde*, Schmidt says, is "the secure archetypal reading of both C and B, emended by R-K from D to *wyde*, which is likely to have come in from *wydewhare* in the previous line (if this seems implausible, their note at p. 165 on what B read is incomprehensible)" (*Parallel-Text*, 378).

16. Paul Eggert, *Securing the Past: Conservation in Art, Architecture and Literature* (Cambridge: Cambridge University Press, 2009), 237.

17. Lee Patterson, *Negotiating the Past: The Historical Understanding of Medieval Literature* (Madison: University of Wisconsin Press, 1987), 113, 112. Perhaps the fullest articulation of the anti-editorial approach is Tim William Machan, *Textual Criticism and Middle English Texts* (Charlottesville: University Press of Virginia, 1994), which for instance sees Kane as reflecting the "self-conscious totalizing that silences opposition and a moral valence recuperated as scientific empiricism" that are two "qualities of traditional textual criticism" (59–60; see 56–64 in general on the Athlone edition); such rhetoric is common in discussions of the Athlone edition.

18. Eggert, *Securing the Past*, 239–40.

19. The claim that the scribe of the Ellesmere and Hengwrt copies of the *Canterbury Tales* copied this manuscript as well appears in Simon Horobin and Linne R. Mooney, "A *Piers Plowman* Manuscript by the Hengwrt/Ellesmere Scribe and Its Implications for London Standard English," *Studies in the Age of Chaucer* 26 (2004): 65–112; his identity as Pinkhurst was put forth in Mooney, "Chaucer's Scribe," *Speculum* 81 (2006): 97–138.

20. See Walter W. Greg, "The Rationale of Copy-Text," in *Collected Papers*, ed. J. C. Maxwell (Oxford: Clarendon, 1966), 381–82, on its role in determining accidentals, never substantives. Kane and Donaldson explain their decision in *The B Version*, 214–15; Schmidt remarks that "each base-manuscript has been preferred less for its superior readings than for its completeness, early date and consistency of grammar and

dialect" (*Parallel-Text*, 260). For discussion of the frequent misconception that copy-text determines substantives, see Joseph A. Dane, "Copy-Text and Its Variants in Some Recent Chaucer Editions," *Studies in Bibliography* 44 (1991): 164–83, and Janet Cowen and George Kane, eds., *Geoffrey Chaucer: "The Legend of Good Women"* (East Lansing, Mich.: Colleagues Press, 1995), 143–49.

21. Kane and Donaldson, *The B Version*, 215 and n181.

22. M. L. Samuels, "Langland's Dialect," *Medium Ævum* 54 (1985): 244. His findings that both A- and B-manuscripts contain relict spellings in that dialect suggest it is very unlikely that, say, B was intended for a London audience and written in the dialect preserved in MS W. Samuels does not prove X's authenticity on this regard, but in my judgment and that of most other critics his argument is convincing enough that it justifies my desire to represent passages from A and B in that language.

23. Ibid., 242.

24. R. W. Chambers, "The Manuscripts of *Piers Plowman* in the Huntington Library, and Their Value for Fixing the Text of the Poem," *Huntington Library Bulletin* 8 (1935): 21.

25. See, e.g., John M. Bowers, "*Piers Plowman*'s William Langland: Editing the Text, Writing the Author's Life," *YLS* 9 (1995): 78–79, and Horobin and Mooney, "A *Piers Plowman* Manuscript," 93–94.

26. Joseph S. Wittig, "*Piers Plowman*": Concordance (London: Athlone, 2001).

27. Cowen and Kane, *The Legend of Good Women*, vii.

28. Ibid., 144.

29. Ibid., 149.

30. "The frequent preservation of multiple authority in the form of drafts, completed manuscripts, typescripts, proofs, as well as variant publication, challenges a critical editor to create an eclectic text that selects the truest authorial characteristics for accidentals from among a body of documents that attest to a variety of possible non-characteristic as well as characteristic forms, not always in series and not always authoritative in the preserved documents of their transmission." Fredson Bowers, "Regularization and Normalization in Modern Critical Texts," *Studies in Bibliography* 42 (1989): 80n3.

31. Dane, "Copy-Text and Its Variants," 170n14 (his emphasis).

32. See Richard Bucci, "Tanselle's 'Editing Without a Copy-Text': Genesis, Issues, Prospects," *Studies in Bibliography* 56 (2003–2004): 1–44 for recent discussion.

CHAPTER 1. *PIERS PLOWMAN* BEFORE 1400: EVIDENCE FOR THE EARLIEST CIRCULATION OF A, B, AND C

1. On 1370 as probable date by which Langland had abandoned or completed A, see Hanna, *William Langland*, 11; George Kane, "Langland, William (c.1325–c.1390)," in *Oxford Dictionary of National Biography*, ed. H. C. G. Matthew and Brian Harrison (Oxford: Oxford University Press, 2004), accessed online; and Schmidt, *Parallel-Text*, 280–81. As will become clear below and in Chapter 2, I reject Jill Mann's argument that

A was produced as an abridgment of the longer versions. "The Power of the Alphabet: A Reassessment of the Relation between the A and the B Versions of *Piers Plowman,*" *YLS* 8 (1994): 21–50.

2. A much longer one separates Chaucer's composition of the *Book of the Duchess* (1360s) from its earliest witnesses (c. 1450), for instance. See Ralph Hanna, *Pursuing History: Middle English Manuscripts and Their Texts* (Stanford, Calif.: Stanford University Press, 1996), 313n6, on the dates of its witnesses.

3. A. I. Doyle, "Remarks on Surviving Manuscripts of *Piers Plowman,*" in *Medieval English Religious and Ethical Literature: Essays in Honour of G. H. Russell,* ed. Gregory Kratzmann and James Simpson (Cambridge: D.S. Brewer, 1986), 36–37. The situation has long been noted; see, e.g., R. W. Chambers and J. H. G. Grattan, "The Text of 'Piers Plowman'," *Modern Language Review* 26 (1931): 36. Noneditors, it seems, paid little attention to such issues, but, we might note, neither did the first substantial argument that the A version was a belated production, Howard Meroney, "The Life and Death of Longe Wille," *ELH* 17 (1950): 1–35. A related claim is David C. Fowler's that early A manuscripts were "read to pieces" by figures of John Ball's temperament because the text was so electrifying. "Star Gazing: Piers Plowman and the Peasants' Revolt," *Review* 18 (1996): 3, 26n3. In my judgment A is no more susceptible to this mode of disappearance than is B or C.

4. Ralph Hanna, "Studies in the Manuscripts of *Piers Plowman,*" *YLS* 7 (1993): 19, also *Pursuing History,* 199, and *William Langland,* 12 (though elsewhere he endorses Doyle's approach: see *Pursuing History,* 235). His primary target among advocates of "extensive hidden circulation" (*William Langland,* 12n44) is not Doyle, but A. G. Rigg and Charlotte Brewer's comment that "there were presumably more A MSS around at the time of the writing of B MSS than vice versa," Rigg and Brewer, eds.,"*Piers Plowman*": *The Z Version* (Toronto: Pontifical Institute of Mediaeval Studies, 1983), 25n73. Together with Hanna, the most influential advocate of this position is Robert Adams: "Surviving copies of A . . . seem noticeably later than we might have expected for a 'first edition'. . . . To conclude, though one cannot place much weight on the slender clues provided by paleography and dialectology, they do at least suggest an alternative hypothesis concerning publication, one that seems fully as likely as the one taken for granted in the Athlone project. Namely, that A (though representing an earlier state of the poem than B) was, because of its fragmentary nature, virtually unknown (may not even have circulated among a coterie) and passed with Langland's other papers and the incomplete C version into the hands of a literary executor," "Editing *Piers Plowman B*: The Imperative of an Intermittently Critical Edition," *Studies in Bibliography* 45 (1992): 61–62. See also, among many others, Mann, "Power," 26; Steven Justice, *Writing and Rebellion: England in 1381* (Berkeley: University of California Press, 1994), 232n130; Kathryn Kerby-Fulton, *Books Under Suspicion: Censorship and Tolerance of Revelatory Writing in Late Medieval England* (Notre Dame, Ind.: University of Notre Dame Press, 2006), 375; George D. Economou, "Chaucer and Langland: A Fellowship of Makers," in *Reading Medieval Culture: Essays in Honor of Robert W. Hanning,* ed. Robert M. Stein and Sandra Pierson Prior (Notre Dame, Ind.: University of Notre Dame Press, 2005), 293–94; and Schmidt, *Parallel-Text,* 91, 273.

5. Hanna, *Pursuing History*, 199; I am drawing as well on "Studies," 19, and *William Langland*, 12 (source of the "certainly fourteenth-century" phrase).

6. Hanna, *Pursuing History*, 313n5. Hanna also cites "the fourteenth-century common ancestor of the B version copies Bodleian Library, MS. Rawlinson poet. 38 (R), and Oxford, Corpus Christi College, MS. 201 (F)," which "replaced its omission of B 3.51–62 with lines dependent on A 3.50–51 (and F includes further unique A intrusions)," since as Chapter 2 will show, RF here actually record a wild version of Bx's reading, with the other tradition taking on new C matter. MS F, which Hanna dates s. xiv ex./xv, does seem to show the influence of the A version (see esp. Adams, "Editing," 51, and Schmidt, *Parallel-Text*, 56, 143–44). But both because the evidence is not incontrovertible (see Kane and Donaldson, *The B Version*, 165–73 for another interpretation of the evidence) and because we cannot know for sure whether the source of contamination is elsewhere identified in our count, I do not include this possible item.

7. Kane, *The A Version*, 78–80, cites 210 errors shared by RU; Schmidt, *Parallel-Text*, 94, cites "219 agreements, about half of them major," showing their descent from a mutual exclusive ancestor.

8. On this matter see Derek Pearsall, "The 'Ilchester' Manuscript of *Piers Plowman*," *Neuphilologische Mitteilungen* 82 (1981): 181–93; Wendy Scase, "Two *Piers Plowman* C-Text Interpolations: Evidence for a Second Textual Tradition," *Notes and Queries* n.s. 34 (1987): 456–63; Hanna, *Pursuing History*, 204–14; Russell and Kane, *The C Version*, 186–94; Andrew Galloway, "Uncharacterizable Entities: The Poetics of Middle English Scribal Culture and the Definitive *Piers Plowman*," *Studies in Bibliography* 52 (1999): 71–74; Kathryn Kerby-Fulton, "Langland 'in His Working Clothes'? Scribe D, Authorial Loose Revision Material, and the Nature of Scribal Intervention," in *Middle English Poetry: Texts and Traditions: Essays in Honour of Derek Pearsall*, ed. A. J. Minnis (York: York Medieval Press, 2001), 139–67; and Schmidt, *Parallel-Text*, 174–75. Scribe D got his name on account of his work on Trinity College Cambridge MS R.3.2, Gower's *Confessio Amantis*, in which he is the fourth of five scribes to contribute; see A. I. Doyle and M. B. Parkes, "The Production of Copies of the *Canterbury Tales* and the *Confessio Amantis* in the Early Fifteenth Century," in *Medieval Scribes, Manuscripts and Libraries: Essays Presented to N. R. Ker*, ed. M. B. Parkes and Andrew G. Watson (London: Scolar, 1978), 163–210, esp. 174–82. On Scribe D's work on the Ilchester MS of *Piers Plowman* see also Kerby-Fulton, "Langland 'in His Working Clothes'?"

9. Hanna, *Pursuing History*, 10.

10. Michael G. Sargent describes the notion "that the numbers of surviving manuscripts do correlate approximately with the number of manuscripts originally copied" as "simple common sense." "What Do the Numbers Mean? A Textual Critic's Observations on Some Patterns of Middle English Manuscript Transmission," in *Design and Distribution of Late Medieval Manuscripts in England*, ed. Margaret Connolly and Linne R. Mooney (York: York Medieval Press, 2008), 212. This might well be true with regard to Middle English works in general, the context for his claim, but Sargent does not address the difficulties of applying this principle on a smaller level, to the *versions* of a poem, or to the question of the order in which such versions achieved readerships. Thus his discussion

of *Piers Plowman* (221–28) seems to suggest that the rebels of 1381 could only have known the C version. While he cites Doyle's claim that "one cannot be content to explain particular predominances in regard to dating, dialect and states of text as solely the results of general factors of destruction, different perils in particular places, or mere chance" (213, quoting "Remarks," 36), he does not note that Doyle's next paragraph identifies a reason for the absence of early A copies, as quoted above, that would not apply to B or C: Doyle does not assume the correlation between surviving copies of versions and those that once existed. One correction is in order as well: Sargent evidently misread Kane and Donaldson's dating of CUL Gg.4.31 (G), *s. xvi*[1] (*The B Version*, 8), as *s. xv*[1] (223n51 and again in 224n58, which repeats all the information from nn 50, 51, 53), with attendant errors in his charts of productions by century (Figures 4 and 5).

11. The following material is based on Schmidt's stemma of A manuscripts (*Parallel-Text*, 93; see 91–113 for discussion), and it accords with Kane's analysis (*The A Version*, 53–114, summarized at 95–97). One item that does not figure in their analyses is MS P (Pembroke College, Cambridge MS 312 C/6), which I consulted in person. Its omission of 7.94–212 (see Kane, 13) suggests a possible affinity with MSS RUE, who place 7.70–212α in their passus 1. Its affiliations are otherwise too diverse to identify any secure genetic relationships, but there are enough errors shared with these three manuscripts, and with the UJ group in passus 7 (Kane, 459), to suggest the possibility that its membership with that group has been obscured by further corruption. Another witness not discussed here is San Marino, Huntington MS Hm 114 (Ht), an early to mid-fifteenth century conflation of all three versions, which in its "more than 160 lines of inserted A text . . . forms 65 agreements, of which the most persistent is with RU." Russell and Kane, *The C Version*, 193; cf. George H. Russell and Venetia Nathan, "A *Piers Plowman* Manuscript in the Huntington Library," *Huntington Library Quarterly* 26 (1963): 122–25, which cites VH as agreeing frequently with Ht; and now John Thorne, "Updating *Piers Plowman* Passus 3: An Editorial Agenda in Huntington Library MS Hm 114," *YLS* 20 (2006): 73–75 on its use of A in that passus.

12. This final item is the only real difference between Schmidt's and Kane's respective stemmata, and it makes no difference to our tally. Schmidt's A-Ø is a copy Langland showed "to personal acquaintances who formed his immediate 'circle' of readers" (*Parallel-Text*, 91), whereas Kane's pre-archetypal copy is the scribal manuscript that Langland used for his B revision (*The A Version*, 463), an idea Schmidt rejects (287). Note that the Z in the list of manuscripts descended from $r^2$ is not "the Z version" but instead $Q^1$, which is what Rigg and Brewer call the straight copy of A 8.89–184 that bridges the Z and C matter (*The Z Version*, 28–30).

13. Its attestation of passages omitted by V shows that British Library MS Harley 875 (H) does not descend from V (Prol.34, 1.103, 1.176–83, 2.56, 2.92, 2.106–21, 2.129, etc.), given the absence of any indication that these readings are the result of correction in H's line of transmission.

14. Kane, *The A Version*, 17; on 165 he refers to V as "manifestly corrupt throughout."

15. Samuels, "Langland's Dialect," 239.

16. Likewise MS J: its genetic relationship with U and Bodley 851's text of A 8.89–184 (Q¹) points to the probable existence of earlier copies, at least one dated to before 1425, and probably much earlier given the complexity of these texts' production and the likelihood that JU's passus 12 plays some role in this relationship (Kane, *The A Version*, 459). Kane identifies MS U as genetically related to MS R alone (78–80, 85), but this does not hold in passus 8, site of only three of RU's 210 agreements in error (1.4 percent; Kane, 79), and seventeen of UJ's forty (42.5 percent; Kane, 76), many of which are shared by Q¹ as well.

17. If these manuscripts descended from the wild and early Z itself they would not be straightforward A copies. On Z's affiliations with **m** see Rigg and Brewer, *The Z Version*, 22–25; see also Hanna, "Studies," 18, 21, and *William Langland*, 38, and George Kane, "The 'Z Version' of *Piers Plowman*," *Speculum* 60 (1985): 916–17. My claim that **m** or its ancestor must pre-date Bodley 851 is definitely true if that document's text is a scribal derivation of A, and only very probably so if it is authorial, in which case its affiliations with **m** would be "archetypal A readings that underwent corruption in **r**" (Schmidt, *Parallel-Text*, 222). According to Schmidt, the hypothetical copy **m** was copied "after the B-Text had been composed, as is indicated by its greater lexical modernisation and by its occasional inclusion from B of Bx readings that seem inauthentic" (92). The earliest surviving witness to this group is London, Society of Antiquaries no. 687 (MS M), c. 1425, which Schmidt places at two removes from **m**, itself a direct copy of Ax. For **m** to be post-1400 we need to imagine that Ax itself lay dormant for a few decades. So even if Z is authorial, it is still easier than not to allow that m was a fourteenth-century production.

18. Carl Grindley, "The A-Version Ancestor of BmBoCot," *YLS* 24 (2010): forthcoming. On this matter see also Kane, *The A Version*, 459, and Bryan P. Davis, "The Rationale for a Copy of a Text: Constructing the Exemplar for British Library Additional MS. 10574," *YLS* 11 (1997): 141–55, whose analysis of the textual affinities differs from Grindley's.

19. Russell and Kane, *The C Version*, 192n2.

20. MS W, *olim* the Duke of Westminster's MS, is now in private hands and has recently been on deposit in York as Borthwick Add. MS 196. I here list these agreements as *A reading] WJ reading*, in the spelling of J: 60 For] *om.* 68 falsnesse] falshede. 69 Lewide men] Þe lewed folc. 70 (And/*Zero*) comen] Þey comen. 82 & leve] *om.* 84 hovide] hoved þer. Support appears in the other agreements shared as well by one other witness or group: 69 levide hym] it leved (J); it lyked (W); hit loved (L). 102 As] *om.* VH. 109 I sauȝ] sagh I RU.

21. If these ratios were consistently maintained over the course of 7200 lines (which is about the length of the B version), W and J would share some 1250 errors, 830 of which would be unique to these two manuscripts. MSS R and F, the most pervasively attested genetic group in B, share only 504 unique errors (Kane and Donaldson, *The B Version*, 25–28; as later chapters will show, many of these "errors" are in fact authorial).

22. Hanna, *Pursuing History*, 235.

23. Adams, "Editing," 62; this assumption of course is necessary to the argument that A manuscripts achieved only belated circulation.

24. See Doyle, "Remarks," 39–42, and Hanna, *William Langland*, 39–40, on the dates of the B manuscripts.

25. Adams, "Editing," 61. Compare Schmidt's B stemma (*Parallel-Text*, 127), which includes four additional pre-1400 copies for reasons to be discussed below.

26. Adams, "Evidence," 174. This stemma relies as well on the findings of Kane and Donaldson, *The B Version*, 57–61, and Schmidt, *Parallel-Text*, 126–52. MS R is Oxford, Bodleian MS Rawlinson poet. 38 (a few leaves are in London, British Library MS Lansdowne 398), and F is Oxford, Corpus Christi College MS 201; the three in β are Oxford, Bodleian MS Laud misc. 581 (L), Trinity College Cambridge MS B.15.17 (W), and Cambridge University Library Dd.1.17 (C); see Hanna, *William Langland*, 14. Other witnesses to B that I do not treat, which do not provide any further evidence of pre-1400 circulation, include the mid-fifteenth-century H (=A's H³), possibly an independent witness to Bx (Kane and Donaldson, 59–61; but cf. Simon Horobin, "Harley 3954 and the Audience of *Piers Plowman*," in *Medieval Texts in Context*, ed. Graham D. Caie and Denis Renevey [New York: Routledge, 2008], 68–84); Ht, whose B matter is a member of the β³ subgroup (Chambers, "Manuscripts," 18); MS S, a mid-sixteenth-century copy affiliated with WHmCr (Kane and Donaldson, 49–50); and a number of sixteenth- and seventeenth-century productions and extracts.

27. Schmidt, *Parallel-Text*, 123, 273 respectively. The former remark continues: "And unless Langland was himself one of John Ball's acquaintances, *Piers Plowman* must be supposed to have been made available to a readership wider than the poet's immediate circle. But for such 'publication' to occur, a copy would have had to be made from his corrected holograph as a basis for further such copies" (123); the latter repeats the claim that "the completed and presumably 'published' B . . . seems more likely [than does A] to have been the version that achieved wide circulation. Its archetypal manuscript was presumably generated only a couple of years before the Rising [of 1381], which some of its ideas and images may have unintentionally inspired (see *Intro*. III, *B*, §§ 1–3)" (273, pointing back to 123). On this basis and his assumption that B 19–20 went on to become C 21–22, Schmidt's stemma of B manuscripts includes three pre-archetypal copies in addition to the C reviser's B manuscript. Neither assumption is well grounded; see below on John Ball and Chapter 4 on the final two passus.

28. See Chapter 3 for Adams's account of the production of B, which does not include the corrupt C reviser's B manuscript. Kane and Donaldson, *The B Version*, 165–73, assert that F alone has 100-odd correct readings from fortuitous variation or correction via consultation of a good (i.e., pre-archetypal) B manuscript; Adams and Schmidt, by contrast, interpret these readings instead as evidence that F was contaminated by an A manuscript (Adams, "Editing," 51; Schmidt, *Parallel-Text*, 56, 143–44); but note that the Athlone editors dismiss that proposal on the grounds that F possesses "intrinsically more authoritative readings in that part of the poem, also, where B's text is unique" (172).

29. Adams, "Editing," 61, citing Samuels, "Langland's Dialect," 240–41.

30. Hanna, *Pursuing History*, 235. Yet while Adams cites B's dialectal layers as evidence for its extensive copying, he tries to explain away very similar indicators in the A tradition: "In his recent study of 'Langland's Dialect,' M. L. Samuels points to a wide

dialect dispersion for the A copies, observing that 'They demonstrate a situation that is found elsewhere in the history of textual criticism, in which the oldest MSS of a work (or their descendants) are found on the periphery of the culture' (238). It should, however, be noted that Samuels is not arguing for A's precedence as the 'first edition' of *Piers*. . . . In reality, this distribution may tell us nothing about the relative antiquity of A's circulation and evince no more than its locus of popularity" ("Editing," 60–61n50).

31. Andrew Galloway remarks that Adams's account of the A version's textual status "explains some peculiar evidence associating A with C rather than B (e.g., AC but no AB spliced texts; AC shared readings), but does not entirely explain the circumstance that led Kane to edit A in a 'rigorously eclectic' manner in the first place: in contrast to both B and C, there is no single reconstructable archetype for A, but rather seven sub-archetypes, suggesting some different process of release than that of C, by most accounts as unfinished at the poet's death as A was" ("Uncharacterizable Entities," 60n3). Adams has recently returned to the topic, citing evidence that "many lateral transfers of complete lines (lines that were original only to a single version) *appear to have moved from B outwards*," remarking that "an extensive study of these small phrasal contaminations between the poem's three versions has recently confirmed my long-held suspicion that the order of the versions' public appearance was probably B > C > A. A clear majority of these interversional corruptions in extant copies moves from B manuscripts outward (perhaps because of B's London connections) mostly toward copies of its genetic ancestor (A), but sometimes also toward copies of its genetic descendant (C)." "The Kane-Donaldson Edition of *Piers Plowman*: Eclecticism's Ultima Thule," *Text* 16 (2006): 136, his emphasis. Yet as Kerby-Fulton says in another context, "the contamination of A texts with B and C lines tells us nothing, given . . . the late date of the most of the A texts," regarding Mann, "Power." Kerby-Fulton, review of *YLS* vol. 8, *Modern Language Review* 93 (1998): 459. And it ignores the evidence of massive movement, both of entire passages and of individual readings, from C outward to Bx, which we will begin to assess in subsequent chapters.

32. George H. Russell, "The Evolution of a Poem: Some Reflections on the Textual Tradition of *Piers Plowman*," *Arts: The Proceedings of the Sydney University Arts Association* 2 (1962): 39; his evidence for wide A readership inheres in the distance, both in time and the textual quality, of surviving A manuscripts from Langland's A. Adams is the only critic I know to have addressed Russell's question ("Editing," 61), but in my judgment his approach to the evidence (i.e., that B achieved widespread early circulation) is much more problematic than Russell's.

33. Russell, "Evolution," 39.

34. Most accounts of Langland's process of self-censorship restrict it to his revisions. Even Kerby-Fulton does not imagine Langland recalling the B version in *Books Under Suspicion* (cf. her speculation that A's association with Uthred explains why he held back on issuing that version, 375).

35. Schmidt speculates "that the poet's death and the release of C" provoked the interest in *Piers Plowman* that arose in the 1390s (*Parallel-Text*, 279), though of course he assumes early circulation of B.

36. On the dialect, codicology, and paleography of these manuscripts see Simon

Horobin, "'In London and Opelond': The Dialect and Circulation of the C Version of *Piers Plowman*," *Medium Ævum* 74 (2005): 248–69. The notion that Langland composed C at the site where these documents would later be produced has been asserted most influentially by Samuels, "Langland's Dialect," which proposes that they indicate Langland's retirement to Malvern, a notion widely repeated but whose logic has never been explained. Derek Pearsall now comments that this suggestion, at least when it identifies the Malvern area as that site, is "not well founded." *"Piers Plowman": A New Annotated Edition of the C-text* (Exeter: University of Exeter Press, 2008), 20–21. But neither is it well founded when it chooses London instead.

37. John M. Bowers, *Chaucer and Langland: The Antagonistic Tradition* (Notre Dame, Ind.: University of Notre Dame Press, 2007), 77, on MS X, citing in addition its "superior textual authority" and status as the product of a scribe with "privileged insider information." Kathryn Kerby-Fulton and Steven Justice cite MS J as "bearing some important marks of proximity to the author," "Scribe D and the Marketing of Ricardian Literature," in *The Medieval Professional Reader at Work: Evidence from Manuscripts of Chaucer, Langland, Kempe, and Gower*, ed. Kathryn Kerby-Fulton and Maidie Hilmo (Victoria, B.C.: University of Victoria, 2001), 217.

38. Schmidt, *Parallel-Text*, 171. Dates of C manuscripts again rely on Doyle, "Remarks," 42–47, and Hanna, *William Langland*, 41–42. Thirteen of the fourteen lost manuscripts are the ancestors of the ten surviving pre-1400 manuscripts. In addition to them, the C copy behind the OLB group, Schmidt's b, is of this era: he comments that "y and b may be assumed to have been coæval" (172). The logic that dates to before 1400 item 6 in the count of A manuscripts and the $\beta^4$ MS in the B stemma above places this copy, too, in that era.

39. It is at least five generations removed: C holograph > Cx > $x^1$ > i > y > XYJ; see Schmidt, *Parallel-Text*, 175–76 (these are his symbols), and Russell and Kane, *The C Version*, 43–44. If Russell and Kane's tentative endorsement of a group [(XY)J], combined with the sense that XH are even closer than XY, as indicated especially by the shared XH readings 1.201 *shit* for *siht* and 2.3 *us* added in another hand as well as their nearly identical presentation of dialect forms, is accurate (46n25), it is up to eight generations removed: C holograph > Cx > $x^1$ > i > y > XHYJ > XHY > XH > X. See also Hanna, "Studies," 1–14, and Horobin, "'In London and Opelond'."

40. Anne Middleton, "Acts of Vagrancy: The C Version 'Autobiography' and the Statute of 1388," in *Written Work: Langland, Labor, and Authorship*, ed. Steven Justice and Kathryn Kerby-Fulton (Philadelphia: University of Pennsylvania Press, 1997), 208–317. Middleton cites the early C circulation in London to support her argument, but does not remark upon the genealogical distance of these London manuscripts from their source (295n8). Not everyone assents to Middleton's argument, though: Schmidt, *Parallel-Text*, 276–77, while finding it "attractive" and acknowledging that it cannot be ruled out, prefers 1386/87 "as the likely date of Langland's death," and Barney, in his review essay on Pearsall, *New Annotated Edition*, pushes the date back much further still, remaining skeptical that C can be confidently dated any time after the Great Schism of 1378. "A Revised Edition of the C Text," *YLS* 23 (2009): 268.

41. Kane, "Langland, William." Kane had earlier expressed his belief that a C manuscript was dated to the first half of the 1380s and that "Langland was dead by 1387" ("The 'Z Version'," 3), and had harshly assessed Middleton's argument. "Langland: Labour and 'Authorship'," *Notes and Queries* n.s. 45 (1998): 424–25, referring to her "disregard of text."

42. Kerby-Fulton, *Books Under Suspicion*, 184 (her translation of the Latin).

43. Ibid., 343–44. *The House of Fame* is cited in John M. Fyler's edition in *The Riverside Chaucer*, gen. ed. Larry D. Benson (Boston: Houghton Mifflin, 1987).

44. Kerby-Fulton, *Books Under Suspicion*, 186.

45. Ralph Hanna, "Emendations to a 1993 'Vita de Ne'erdowel'," *YLS* 14 (2000): 188, referring to Justice, *Writing and Rebellion*, as discussed below.

46. Greg Walker's judgment regarding Frank Grady, "Chaucer Reading Langland: *The House of Fame*," *Studies in the Age of Chaucer* 18 (1996): 3–23, as discussed below, in Alan J. Fletcher, Elaine M. Treharne, and Walker, "Middle English: Excluding Chaucer," *Year's Work in English Studies* 77 (1996): 190.

47. Respectively, Léopold Hervieux, ed., *Les Fabulistes Latins: Depuis le siècle d'Auguste jusqu' à la fin du moyen âge*, vol. 4, *Eudes de Cheriton et ses dérivés* (1896; New York: Georg Olms Verlag, 1970), 243 (this is in Langland's form, *esses*); Kerby-Fulton, *Books Under Suspicion*, 451n58, citing John A. Alford, *"Piers Plowman": A Guide to the Quotations* (Binghamton, N.Y.: Medieval and Renaissance Texts and Studies, 1992), 78 (this is in "Heu"'s form, *fuisses*, though it would not be surprising if this turned into *esses* in some manuscripts and sermons).

48. See *Middle English Dictionary*, s.v. "wer(e" (n.5), 1.a, and George Kane, *"Piers Plowman": Glossary* (New York: Continuum, 2005), s.v. "weer."

49. As Kerby-Fulton acknowledges: *Books Under Suspicion*, 343.

50. J. A. W. Bennett, *Chaucer's "Book of Fame": An Exposition of "The House of Fame"* (Oxford: Clarendon, 1968), 92.

51. Ralph Hanna and Traugott Lawler, eds., *Boece*, 1.pr5.74–76 in *The Riverside Chaucer*; cf. 1.pr6.97–100.

52. Cowen and Kane, *The Legend of Good Women*, lines 2683–86.

53. Grady, "Chaucer Reading Langland." For three indicators of its impact, see Fletcher, Treharne, and Walker, "Middle English," 190, as cited above; Hanna, "Emendations," 191; and Horobin and Mooney, "A *Piers Plowman* Manuscript," 101.

54. Helen Cooper, "Langland's and Chaucer's Prologues," *YLS* 1 (1987): 74. See Derek Pearsall, *The Life of Geoffrey Chaucer: A Critical Biography* (Oxford: Blackwell, 1992), 227, 337n3 on the date of the *General Prologue*.

55. Grady has it that "each poet resigns in what looks like frustration" ("Chaucer Reading Langland," 20); while Cooper notes that "the one further analysis of society Langland wrote, the episode of Piers's and Grace's assignment of social roles in the Dobest section, is the only one that has no precise parallels in Chaucer, and it is, of course, found only in the B and C texts, not in A" ("Langland's and Chaucer's Prologues," 76). The only hope for reconciliation of the two approaches would be to say that Chaucer first read *Piers Plowman* A, then wrote the *General Prologue*, then read B, then wrote the *House*

*of Fame.* Cooper's separate redating of the *House of Fame* to a later era, when the influence of Boethius became manifest, could nourish such a chronology; see "The Four Last Things in Dante and Chaucer: Ugolino in the House of Rumour," *New Medieval Literatures* 3 (1999): 59. In any case, Kathryn L. Lynch judges Cooper's argument "both methodologically and factually shaky," since the very early *Parliament of Fowls*, too, shows Boethius's influence. "Dating Chaucer," *Chaucer Review* 42 (2007): 18n28.

56. Economou, "Chaucer and Langland," 293, continuing at 294; ironically his target is Cooper, "Langland's and Chaucer's Prologues."

57. E.g., Donaldson, *C-Text*, 108; Justice, *Writing and Rebellion*, 231–51; Schmidt, *Parallel Text*, 273.

58. London, B.L. MS Royal 13 E IX, fol. 287r, as quoted in Richard Firth Green, "John Ball's Letters: Literary History and Historical Literature," in *Chaucer's England: Literature in Historical Context*, ed. Barbara Hanawalt (Minneapolis: University of Minnesota Press, 1992), 195.

59. Especially Justice, as discussed below, and nearly everyone who has mentioned the topic in his wake; an earlier instance is Elizabeth Kirk, who says that it is "well known" that Ball relied upon B. "Langland's Plowman and the Recreation of Fourteenth-Century Religious Metaphor," *YLS* 2 (1988): 11. The main recent exceptions are Anne Hudson, "*Piers Plowman* and the Peasants' Revolt: A Problem Revisited," *YLS* 8 (1994): 85–106; Cooper, "Langland's and Chaucer's Prologues," 73–74 and n4; and Fowler, "Star Gazing." The former two were written before Justice's book; the latter is a review of that book. Both Hudson and Fowler date B to after the revolt.

60. Schmidt, *Parallel-Text*, 276, where he also identifies still other "echoes" and discusses the Carter letter along the same lines.

61. In the *Ego dormio*, Barry Windeatt, ed., *English Mystics of the Middle Ages* (Cambridge: Cambridge University Press, 1994), 25.

62. Kane, "Langland, William."

63. Ibid. If we are to find echoes between these two texts, it would have to be in the other direction, if the argument of Chapter 4 below is correct. After all, Langland's knowledge of Ball's letters is the single factor behind the production of C upon which everyone agrees.

64. Quotations from the Bible are from the Challoner revision of the Douay-Rheims translation, *The Holy Bible* (1899; Rockford, Ill.: Tan Books, 1989); the Vulgate is from *Biblia Sacra: Iuxta Vulgatam Versionem*, ed. Robert Weber, 3rd ed. (Stuttgart: Deutsche Bibelgesellschaft, 1983).

65. Justice, *Writing and Rebellion*, 102, 105.

66. On *mamzer* as "bastard" see James A. Brundage, *Law, Sex, and Christian Society in Medieval Europe* (Chicago: University of Chicago Press, 1987), 55.

67. As pointed out by Fowler, "Star Gazing," 8, who call this Justice's " 'open, sesame!' for entering the text of *Piers Plowman*."

68. Justice, *Writing and Rebellion*, 106 (quotations, including translation of the Latin; Justice's italics), 129.

69. "Wit's denunciation of bishops thus lands (in Ball's sermon) in the middle of a

disendowment proposal, where Langland never meant it to be: Wit himself imagines no remedy more profound than a better crop of bishops" (ibid., 106).

70. Isabel Davis, *Writing Masculinity in the Later Middle Ages* (Cambridge: Cambridge University Press, 2007), 22–24.

71. John A. Alford says Langland "drew upon the commentaries and upon some such work as Bromyard's (if not the *Summa Praedicantium* itself) for the majority of his quotations," continuing: "The possibility that Langland was influenced by Bromyard is improved by recent scholarship on the dating of the *Summa*" to c. 1348–50. "The Role of the Quotations in *Piers Plowman*," *Speculum* 52 (1977): 99 and n60. I consulted Bromyard in London, British Library MS Royal 7 E IV, fol. 296r–v.

72. Hudson, "*Piers Plowman* and the Peasants' Revolt," 88 (though she notes that something might have been lost in the text of Ball's letter here); likewise Cooper six years earlier, "Langland's and Chaucer's Prologues," 73–74n4; and Fowler, "Star Gazing," 7.

73. Mann, "Power," 40n22.

74. Green, "John Ball's Letters," 185.

75. Margaret Aston, "Corpus Christi and Corpus Regni: Heresy and the Peasants' Revolt," *Past and Present* 143 (1994): 26. The "Hob the Robber" reference is to the line "Competenter per Robert, robbur designatur," from "Song of the Times" in Harley 978, *Thomas Wright's Political Songs of England: From the Reign of John to that of Edward II*, ed. Peter Cross (1839; Cambridge: Cambridge University Press, 1996), 49; see also Walter W. Skeat, ed., *The Vision of William Concerning Piers the Plowman: In Three Parallel Texts*, 2 vols. (1886; Oxford: Oxford University Press, 1969), 2:88 (n. to his C 7.316, Russell and Kane's 6.315). Elizabeth Kirk has argued that Langland's plowman is "radically new" ("Langland's Plowman," 12), but Aston's objection cannot be dismissed out of hand; Derek Pearsall's 2008 revision of his edition of the C text still maintains "that *Peres* and *plouhman* were a traditional collocation" (*New Annotated Edition*, 149, n. to C 7.200), despite the claims of Kirk, whose work he discusses elsewhere in the edition (33).


CHAPTER 2. SCRIBAL CONFLATION, CONVERGENT VARIATION,
AND THE INVENTION OF *PIERS PLOWMAN* B


1. Fortescue copied MS Digby 145, K of A and D² of C. See Thorlac Turville-Petre, "Sir Adrian Fortescue and his Copy of *Piers Plowman*," *YLS* 14 (2000): 29–48.

2. C. L. Wrenn, review of Kane, *The A Version*, *Modern Language Notes* 76 (1961): 858. Thirty-five years later Charlotte Brewer would repeat the sentiment: after a two-page summary of this chapter, she remarks: "Kane's third chapter, entitled 'Classification of the Manuscripts,' moves on to the meat of his Introduction." *Editing "Piers Plowman": The Evolution of the Text* (Cambridge: Cambridge University Press, 1996), 358; see also Hanna's characterization of Kane's third chapter as the edition's real beginning in "George Kane."

3. Kane, *The A Version*, 28. The seven manuscripts comprise the TH²Ch group;

Harley 3954, which begins with B material and then becomes A; and the three to which we now turn.

4. Kane, *The A Version*, 29, 32 (with the latter matter repeated, 33).

5. National Library of Wales MS 733B, p. 6.

6. Kane, *The A Version*, 32.

7. He discusses five of WN's twelve conflated passages, five of W's sixteen, four of N's nine (plus a continuation, by N alone, of a WN conflation he had discussed earlier), and two of K's thirteen (31–38).

8. The Latin lines, all attested by MS W as well, are C 1.140α after A 1.132, C 1.174α after A 1.152, C 1.183α after A 1.161, C 2.81 after A 2.56, and C 3.190α after A 3.141. The two other lines are C 6.367 after A 5.162, with VHEAMH³, and C 6.373 after A 5.165, with VHMH³. It is in theory possible that the middle three of the Latin tags, and the two lines in passus 5, came from a B source, as Kane says, but given the lack of any other evidence that N conflates from B that seems unlikely (the one seeming exception will occupy us in detail below).

9. WN's "I ou3t ben herre þan she for I come of a better," Kane's A 2.21, is substantively identical to C 2.30, for which Russell and Kane's text reads "Y ouhte ben herrore than he; y com of a bettere." The only substantive variant (since "he" is a dialectal rendering of "she") appears to be the absence of "for" in C, but in fact MSS VHJLK of A omit this term, while MSS P² and M of C include it.

10. National Library of Wales MS 733B, p. 3.

11. Ibid., pp. 15–16. Kane identifies the conflated passage as B 3.51–62 or C 3.56–66 (*The A Version*, 30 and apparatus at 3.50–51), that is, excluding the final bold line, but it is quite clearly the W-M passage and not C's. It is unclear why Kane thinks N returns to A at line 3.52; it makes much more sense to take its final line as continuing W-M (3.63) than as returning to A before the passage has ended. Donaldson had interpreted the situation thus as well ("MSS R and F," 209).

12. See Russell and Nathan, "A *Piers Plowman* Manuscript in the Huntington Library."

13. Kane, *The A Version*, 42.

14. Russell and Kane, *The C Version*, 119; also Kane and Donaldson, *The B Version*, 116–17.

15. Kane and Donaldson, *The B Version*, 220.

16. E. Talbot Donaldson, *Speaking of Chaucer* (New York: Norton, 1970), 107.

17. Kane, *The A Version*, 82.

18. Russell and Kane, *The C Version*, 59.

19. Kane, *The A Version*, 62.

20. A summary of the situation, including expressions of these judgments, appears in Adams's justly influential essay "Editing *Piers Plowman* B."

21. Kane and Donaldson, *The B Version*, 70 (on Bx), 98 (on the C reviser's B manuscript); see 70–97 on the former, 98–127 on the latter.

22. Ibid., 129.

23. As in, for instance, Jerome McGann, *Radiant Textuality: Literature After the*

*World Wide Web* (New York: Palgrave Macmillan, 2001), 75–77 (under the influence of his former colleague Lee Patterson's "Logic of Textual Criticism," *Negotiating the Past*, 77–113), where "the Kane-Donaldson project is a gage laid down, a challenge to scholars to imagine what they know or think they know about certain complex materials and disciplinary procedures" (77).

24. Brewer, *Editing*, 348. The notion that "the Z version" is authorial, after all, both relies upon and has as its biggest implication the idea that many more of the individual lectional variations, even within manuscripts of the same version (especially the A tradition), are authorial than the Athlone edition allows.

25. Respectively, Adams, "Editing," and Mann, "Power." Ralph Hanna, Sean Taylor, and Steven Justice have independently argued that the RF manuscripts represent a separate stage in the production of *Piers Plowman*, an approach that does focus on shapes and paragraph-length passages rather than individual lections. But such arguments, too, reinscribe the authorial status of the surviving shapes, simply identifying more authorial shapes than do Kane and his colleagues. Hanna, *Pursuing History*, 215–29; Taylor, "The Lost Revision of *Piers Plowman B*," *YLS* 11 (1997): 97–134; and Justice, "Introduction: Authorial Work and Literary Ideology," in Justice and Kerby-Fulton, *Written Work*, 5–8.

26. This is Crowley's first edition (Cr¹), in the Lehigh University copy, 821.1 L265p 1550, sig. *iiv, Frontmatter 11 in the online facsimile. Crowley himself might have written the wordlist in Cambridge University Library MS Ll.4.14 (C² of B); see J. R. Thorne and Marie-Claire Uhart, "Robert Crowley's *Piers Plowman*," *Medium Ævum* 55 (1986): 248–54. In examining copies of Crowley's 1550 and Owen Rogers's 1561 editions, I have found that such lists were very common in added flyleaves up through the nineteenth century; see my note "The Gentleman's *Piers Plowman*: John Mitford and his Annotated Copy of the 1550 Edition of William Langland's Great Poem," *La Trobe Journal* 84 (2009): 108–10 for discussion. This phenomenon culminates in the magisterial *Concordance* by Joseph Wittig, *Glossary* by Kane, and "Indexical Glossary" by Schmidt (*Parallel-Text*, 753–914).

27. Mann, "Power," 27; here she also says, though, that "it is only when we can scan the whole corpus of manuscript variants, and work with an edition which has been established by critically weighing all of them, that we can be reasonably sure of avoiding the distortion likely to arise when using an edition which largely represents a single manuscript." See also Bowers, "*Piers Plowman*'s William Langland," 86–90, for the proposal that A was an abridgment of the longer versions.

28. For similar observations with regard to the practical limitations of the Athlone edition, see Hoyt N. Duggan, "Creating an Electronic Archive of *Piers Plowman*," 1994 (online), section on "Producing a Critical Text." Tim William Machan aligns this procedure of Kane and Donaldson's with "the New Critical separation of literary texts from cultural contexts" (*Textual Criticism*, 59). On the theoretical underpinnings of lemmatization see also Hanna, *Pursuing History*, 64–66.

29. The material common to MSS J and Ht discussed below shows the feasibility of this idea, my own arguments aside.

30. Mann, "Power," 46.

31. Ibid., 35.

32. Ibid.

33. Kane and Donaldson, assuming that RF and the rest of the B manuscripts witness an identical archetype, say that RF "omit" lines 182–88. They defend that assumption in their introduction, where they characterize this as an instance of homeoarchy (*maner . . . man* 182, *man and womman* 189) (*The B Version*, 68). Donaldson had discussed the RF manuscripts' assimilation to A in his major 1955 essay ("MSS R and F," 209), but he and Kane nowhere mention this effect of RF's "omission."

34. Russell and Kane's apparatus for line 285 includes some of the same material in the variants for both "a" and "a(2)." To clarify, I have added a "(2)" to the first of these, and omitted the second. Their entry for "worcheth" in line 288 neglects to include $N^2$ in the list of witnesses to that term, and their entry "tolde] 30w tolde XYUN$^2$" in line 289 is incorrect since, as their apparatus correctly indicates earlier in the line, this phrase is absent from $N^2$.

35. Respectively, Kane and Donaldson, *The B Version*, 67–68; Hanna, *Pursuing History*, 217.

36. The presence of these spurious lines in RF is part of the evidence that it cannot have been a much earlier production than W-M, as the next chapter will demonstrate.

37. The first three lines are from Kane and Donaldson, *The B Version*, 221 (punctuation added); the last is my reconstruction of RF's text from their apparatus at B 3.63, where they identify RF as resuming and in which they treat its agreements with A for *ech* and *see* (F; R: *Ise*) as against W-M's *man* and *seye* as evidence of the authorial B reading.

38. The differences between W-M/$N^2$ and Cx occur in B272/C288, where Cx reads "And" for "Y" (Russell-Kane adopt $N^2$'s reading), and B273/C289 where Cx omits "forth" and reads "we" for "he" (Kane-Donaldson emend to "we").

39. Kane and Donaldson, *The B Version*, 224 (punctuation added).

40. There are 247 $N^2$/W-M agreements, comprising sixty-four with Bx (sixty-one shared with RF and three in a single line omitted from RF via eyeskip, as is clear from the line's necessity to context [B 17.320/C 19.300]), ninety-three where RF=Cx, eighty-five among the eighty-one lines and passages discussed here, and five where RF is wild or deficient. There are also four readings where $N^2$ agrees with RF alone, of which only one very minor instance occurs where W-M is attested (*om.* "þat" at B 18.69/C 20.71). For details see Warner, "The Ur-B *Piers Plowman* and the Earliest Production of C and B," *YLS* 16 (2002): 3–39, esp. 7n11, 29–36.

41. Russell and Kane, *The C Version*, 102n23, where they catalogue forty-five readings for which they adopt unique $N^2$ readings where what they claim to be Bx is available as a control. In fact they adopt $N^2$ fifty-one times: to their list add 10.6, 10.85, 11.307, 20.132, 20.208, and 20.264. They do not note that RF supports only twenty-eight of these fifty-one supposed Bx readings.

42. See Schmidt, *Parallel-Text*, 185–86. Hanna maintains that $N^2$ is a "B-conflated A+C copy": *London Literature, 1300–1380* (Cambridge: Cambridge University Press, 2005), 246, and see now his "George Kane and the Invention of Textual Thought," in which, like Schmidt, he does not mention RF's role in the problem, instead offering a few

alternative explanations for some features of the overall problem treated in isolation, as well as some observations with which I agree but that have no bearing on the issue. For instance, he says that the evidence that other manuscript readings appear in $N^2$ means that it developed very late in the transmission process and thus, he claims, cannot witness to early-stage Langlandian poetry. But this conclusion does not follow from the premise (which itself is manifestly true). $N^2$'s wildness is not a guarantee against Nx's privileged status: Hanna is conflating two separate stages of production. By his logic, we could not call $N^2$ a copy of the C text at all, since by "C" we mean early-stage Langlandian poetry. In any case, the sites where Nx agrees with W-M are of an entirely different order from those where it agrees in error with the manuscripts Hanna cites. They occur, to repeat, often over entire passages, for some 250 readings, three-quarters of which are for lections or entire passages where RF of B is spurious or absent.

43. See Schmidt, *Parallel-Text*, 185–86, discussing ten W-M readings in $N^2$ that Russell and Kane adopt in their C text, but that he rejects from B in favor of the RF-Cx reading (i.e., among the ninety-three such readings). Schmidt nowhere mentions the fact that $N^2$ agrees with W-M for entire passages for which RF attests nothing, and users of his edition cannot deduce its existence because "$N^2$ is only selectively cited" in his apparatus (186).

44. See Robert Adams, "The R/F MSS of *Piers Plowman* and the Pattern of Alpha/Beta Complementary Omissions: Implications for Critical Editing," *Text* 14 (2002): 114, on this statistic, which a glance at Kane and Donaldson's apparatus will confirm.

45. Doyle, "Remarks," 46.

46. The most distinctive terms are "þorow" *through*, "worche" *work*, and "nouʒt" *not*, whose use together points to Warwickshire as most likely site of the scribe's linguistic home, according to my interpretation of the evidence found in Angus McIntosh, M. L. Samuels, and Michael Benskin, eds., *A Linguistic Atlas of Late Mediaeval English*, 4 vols. (Aberdeen: Aberdeen University Press, 1986). The A and C texts are not strongly differentiated, suggesting the likelihood that this is the scribe's language, though of course this scribe might well have simply faithfully copied his exemplar. I will present a full linguistic analysis in my forthcoming edition of the manuscript for the *Piers Plowman Electronic Archive*.

47. On pp. 14, 75, 107 (the only with the "capellanus" item), and 137. Only the final item has been noticed (Doyle, "Remarks," 46n43), where it is recorded as "Staptun," but both this and the site of his chaplaincy are extraordinarily difficult to decipher, even under ultra-violet light. I would welcome any help in identifying this individual.

48. Kane, *The A Version*, 12.

49. Ibid., 43.

50. Scase, "Two *Piers Plowman* C-Text Interpolations," argues that the C material common to Ht and J (in the variant lines added to the latter's Prologue) attests an earlier stage of authorial production; Russell and Kane have now asserted that Ht shares some eighty C readings with $N^2$ over 370-odd lines (*The C Version*, 102n23), saying that "it seems possible that Ht's source of C material here and $N^2$'s exemplar were gemels" (193n7).

51. Kane, *The A Version*, 44.

CHAPTER 3. THE POISON OF POSSESSION: B PASSUS 15

1. On the Donation of Constantine see Pearsall, *New Annotated Edition*, 291, note to C 17.220, and especially Alfred Hiatt, *The Making of Medieval Forgeries: False Documents in Fifteenth-Century England* (London: The British Library; Toronto: University of Toronto Press, 2004), 136–55.

2. Wycliffism: Pearsall as in previous note; Pamela Gradon, "Langland and the Ideology of Dissent," *Proceedings of the British Academy* 66 (1980): 186–88, and Anne Hudson, *The Premature Reformation: Wycliffite Texts and Lollard History* (Oxford: Clarendon, 1988), 405–6. Anticlericalism: Wendy Scase, *"Piers Plowman" and the New Anticlericalism* (Cambridge: Cambridge University Press, 1989), 109–12. Franciscanism: Aubrey Gwynn, "The Date of the B-Text of *Piers Plowman*," *Review of English Studies* 19 (1943): 11–12, 17–18; Lawrence Clopper builds upon Gwynn's ideas, citing 15.551–64 among other lines, in *"Songes of Rechelesnesse": Langland and the Franciscans* (Ann Arbor: University of Michigan Press, 1997), 160–66. Vernacularism: Fiona Somerset, *Clerical Discourse and Lay Audience in Late Medieval England* (Cambridge: Cambridge University Press, 1998), 53–54. English historiography: Emily Steiner, "Radical Historiography: Langland, Trevisa, and the *Polychronicon*," *Studies in the Age of Chaucer* 27 (2005): 210–11; 15.564 is her epigraph (171). David Aers makes the point that the retention of these lines in C undermines that version's reputation as a defensive poem in political retreat from the radical nature of B: review of Justice and Kerby-Fulton, *Written Work*, YLS 12 (1998): 212, on Kerby-Fulton's "Bibliographic Ego" (67–143).

3. National Library of Wales MS 733B, pp. 125–26. I have silently expanded abbreviations. Line numbers in the left margin are keyed to B 15/C 17, and appear before and after each of the four C lines omitted by both texts, as well as at the first line and before the site of the eighteen-line C-only passage, which N² includes but I do not print. Readings in brackets are my corrections to N² and are restricted to omission of terms (*3e* 548/210; *3oure* 551/214; *þo* 561/224) or spelling errors (N² reads *vos* at 552/215, 560/223; *3it* at 553/216), which have no bearing on the pattern I am discussing; the angle brackets at 552–52α/215–15α indicate rearrangement of lines, as N² places the Latin tag in the margin after 551/214. Final C readings for each item in bold, and the lines not in N²/W-M, are: 533/194 riht holy. 536/197 here Consience. 538/199 *transposed*. 540/201 byfore; and resceyved. 202 To amende and to make as with men of holy churche. 546/208 clerkes. 547/209 overturne. 548/210 Minne. 212 How tho corsede cristene catel and richesse worschipede. 550/213 dampnede. 551/214 clerkes; come auht longe. 552/215 dampne; depose 30w for 3oure pruyde. 553/216 þe comune. 554/217 *om.* 555/218 lese 3e shal for ever. 556/219 dede and as. 557/220 his cortesye. 562/225 moste; myhte; þe prelates. 563/226 and possession. 228 Yf the kynges coveyte in cristes pees to lyuene. 565/229 For if. 230 The hevedes of holy churche and tho that ben under hem. 566/231 Hit were charite. 567/232 þe olde poysen. 568/250 and preyede thus the. 569/251 now cristes.

4. Anne Hudson, "Langland and Lollardy?" *YLS* 17 (2003): 93.

5. Hudson, *"Piers Plowman* and the Peasants' Revolt," 101.

6. Gwynn, "Date," 12.

7. Gradon, "Ideology," 188.

8. Gwynn, "Date," 12.

9. Kane and Donaldson, *The B Version*, 176.

10. Ibid., 176–79 (reconstruction), 116 (C reviser's B MS).

11. A. V. C. Schmidt adopts the Kane-Donaldson reconstruction (see *Parallel-Text*, 432), Pearsall calls their analysis "most astute" (review of Kane and Donaldson, *Medium Ævum* 46 [1977]: 283), and Robert Adams describes it as "completely convincing" ("R/F MSS," 118), though as we shall see he disagrees with their explanation for how the error occurred. For demurrals see David C. Fowler, "A New Edition of the B Text of *Piers Plowman*," *Yearbook of English Studies* 7 (1977): 37, though even he "commend[s] it to the reader for its logic, ingenuity, and honesty in argument," and Clopper, *"Songes"*, 276 and n18.

12. Kane and Donaldson, *The B Version*, 177–78.

13. Ibid., 178n101.

14. See discussion in Chapter 2. Another idea would be that these lines had not yet been revised from B to their final C form when Nx was produced. This would need to accept as a given my premise that Nx was an early and independent witness to C, which would already prevent its acceptance by those attempting to argue that $N^2$ bears witness only to late stages of C (as does Hanna). That aside, until deep in his revision of B passus 18 Langland never allowed so many lines to remain untouched (see Chapter 4 below on the seeming absence of revision in the final two passus). It seems unbelievable that he would add eighteen lines (see next note) but not even look at the other forty. Nx's status as an early witness to C is indeed the best explanation for the sixty-odd individual readings it shares with Bx (i.e., with both W-M and RF), but the agreements at issue, unlike those Bx/Nx ones, are not isolated, local readings but rather whole lines or passages. In Donaldson's estimation, only 37 percent of the lines of the B-continuation appear in the same form in C (*C-Text*, 22).

15. The most powerful indicator that lines 233–49 were not omitted from W-M via eyeskip between "For were presthode more parfyte" (233) and "Yf presthode were parfyt and preyede thus" (250), which otherwise would be a reasonable idea, is the addition of the phrase "and preyede thus" in 250, which manifestly points back to the previous eighteen lines ("His *preyeres* with his pacience to pees sholde brynge" 236; the pope, prelates, and priests must "*preeye* and biseche / Devouteliche day and nyhte" 244–45), clearly intended to smooth the incorporation of the new lines. It would be quite a coincidence if W-M happened to omit both the passage and this transitional phrase and left no indications of his errors. In addition, line 236, just quoted, so I will argue in the Conclusion, is part of C 17's program of reworking the draft material that ended up as B 15.417–28α (here, line 427, "Hir preyeres and hir penaunces to pees sholde brynge"). There is also precedent for the phenomenon of Langland's addition of passages by reusing the line at the site of the insertion, such as the repetition of C 3.115 (=B 3.87), "Ac Mede þe mayde þe mayre a bisowte," at C 3.77, "3ut mede the mayr myldeliche he bysouhte," which inaugurates the new passage C 3.77–114 (but cf. Russell and Kane, *The C Version*, 86, for a different explanation).

16. Donaldson, "MSS R and F," 209.

17. Ibid., 210.

18. Ibid., 210–11. I have retained Skeat's line numbers because the order of the received text is Donaldson's topic, adding Kane and Donaldson's line numbers for the sake of convenience and because they indicate at a glance the effects of the Athlone reconstruction. The line numbers of C are the same, and I have normalized the passus number of the C lines from Skeat's 18 to the Athlone 17. I also change Donaldson's "later" to "latter" in the final phrase, as there is good reason to suspect this of being an error of transmission (the essay has quite a few typographical errors).

19. The proposal that RF is transitional between B and C, says Andrew Galloway, "finds abundant confirmation and appears likely to constitute a permanent change to the paradigm that Langland scholarship for another period will generally accept" ("Uncharacterizable Entities," 69, referring to Hanna, *Pursuing History*, 215–29; Taylor, "Lost Revision"; and Justice, "Introduction," 5–8). See Skeat, *Vision of William*, 2:lxviii for the originary statement of this belief. Among these critics only Hanna mentions RF's assimilation to A: "these omissions (B 8.14–17; 9.163–64, 182–88, 202–6) plausibly exemplify homeoarchy (so *Piers Plowman: The B Version* 67–68); alternatively, they could reflect a state of the text where the scribe simply missed some brief revisions (e.g., on loose sheets temporarily separated from copy)" (*Pursuing History*, 217). The former explanation would be an extraordinary coincidence (especially now that $N^2$'s readings are available); the latter needs Bx to have authorial status (see further below). Hanna later says that he ratifies Donaldson's belief that there are two stages to B, "although at that time, Donaldson believed, on the basis of a very few passages, [W-M] to represent the later stage of the text" (223); but even if this forty-line passage were Donaldson's sole instance, his argument is stronger on its own terms than is the idea that RF attest rolling B > C revision. Both Hanna and Taylor cite the fact that RF's "omitted" lines appear throughout the text, whereas W-M's are focused upon passus 11–17 (Hanna, 220; Taylor, 102–4), but the appearance of $N^2$ throws this out of whack: RF's omissions, too, are concentrated in the middle portion of the poem. See my "Ur-B *Piers Plowman*," 20.

20. Adams, "R/F MSS," 121. In this scenario the resulting mess mightily confused subsequent scribes: the W-M scribe guessed poorly as to the location of 533–69, while the RF scribe in turn omitted the passage because he took offense at it, assumed it had been canceled, never saw it, or, like W-M, lacked an insertion marker and did not know where it belonged, but unlike him did not hazard a guess (122).

21. Ibid., 118, citing findings and opinions by Richard Beadle and Ian Doyle.

22. Adams, "R/F MSS," 115 (quotation only).

23. Donaldson, "MSS R and F," 184.

24. Adams, "R/F MSS," 121.

25. Ibid., 128, 129. Adams does not mention that the former passages bring RF perfectly into line with A in passus 8 and 9, which had driven Donaldson's essay; he simply endorses Kane and Donaldson's analyses. See also Hanna, *Pursuing History*, 217, as discussed above.

26. Russell and Kane, *The C Version*, 89. In his review of Russell and Kane, Adams comments, "for the first time in the long history of this project, the editors acknowledge

(pp. 86–89) that a major factor in some of the textual anomalies of the extant *Piers Plowman* manuscripts was Langland's habit of adding afterthoughts and revisions in long marginals or crabbed interlinears, on separate leaves and even on small scraps of parchment (all easily overlooked or mispositioned)," *Speculum* 74 (1999): 1085.

27. Pearsall, "The 'Ilchester' Manuscript," 185; Scase, "Two *Piers Plowman* C-Text Interpolations," arguing (as opposed to Pearsall) that this is early-draft authorial material, as implicitly endorsed by Russell and Kane, *The C Version*, 186–94. For my purposes here it does not matter whether this is authorial or scribal.

28. Kane and Donaldson, *The B Version*, 176; Donaldson, "MSS R and F," 209.

29. This is my reconstruction of Langland's original here. Lines 527–28 are in RF only, and I present the rest as they appear in W-M, since Kane and Donaldson adopt many RF/Cx readings which, I argue below, are C contaminations of RF, meaning that W-M's text is much closer to the ur-B text. I transpose the final two terms of 571, as does C, on metrical grounds (i.e., so as to end with a trochee, as it were).

30. The fact that rhetoric so firmly associated with the Becket legendary both precedes and follows these lines supports my contention that the absence of 511–28 from W-M is the result of eyeskip: the figure of St. Thomas would have generated this portion of the poem, rather than being an afterthought. See Warner, "Becket and the Hopping Bishops," *YLS* 17 (2003): 107–34.

31. Kane and Donaldson, *The B Version*, 177.

32. Ibid., 179n104.

33. I give M's text (consulted in London), fol. 70r–v. The term "prestes" in line 188 comes from the ancestor of MSS PERMVA (Schmidt's m group); all other manuscripts read "prelates," as in line 260. In fact the textual situation of M is more complex than Kane and Donaldson's description of it as simple transposition suggests: it reads 17.186, 286, 187, 259–85β (the entry for these lines in Russell and Kane's apparatus should include the Latin and read "copied after 187," not 186), 188–258, 287. Schmidt attributes M's mangled text here to "mechanical causes" (he does not mention the possibility of eyeskip): "Though interesting, therefore, M's witness is unlikely to have any bearing on the arguments for re-ordering B 504–69" (*Parallel-Text*, 432). Both Russell-Kane and Schmidt say that M's dislocations are noted in the manuscript, but I saw no signs of such marks. I suspect these editors did not notice that the signs they took to indicate displacement appeared on every folio of the manuscript as well, intended for the rubricator.

34. "Those bishops bearing the names of foreign places had dimly penetrated his consciousness, and on returning to work he accidentally traveled from Bethlehem and Babylon to Syria" ("MSS R and F," 206; also Kane and Donaldson, *The B Version*, 67). See below for other, to my mind unconvincing, explanations.

35. The ten appearances of *riche* and its cognates that would result between lines 324–43α/533–44 would be among the densest in the poem. Wittig's *Concordance* shows that as a passus B 14 is densest, with thirty-one appearances of *riche* or *richesse*, including eight in lines 140–57. Langland clearly relished such intensity.

36. M. Teresa Tavormina, "*Piers Plowman* and the Liturgy of St. Lawrence: Composition and Revision in Langland's Poetry," *Studies in Philology* 84 (1987): 268. Her point

is apt, if overstated: Thomas Becket, too, was invoked as an enemy of possession, even by Wyclif. See Warner, "Becket," 109–10.

37. Mary Carruthers, *The Search for St. Truth: A Study of Meaning in "Piers Plowman"* (Evanston, Ill.: Northwestern University Press, 1973), 126. Likewise Elizabeth D. Kirk and Judith H. Anderson describe line 347 as the point from which "Anima's discourse on Charity becomes generalized to include various subjects whose connection with his original theme must be inferred by the reader," *"Piers Plowman": An Alliterative Verse Translation by E. Talbot Donaldson* (New York: Norton, 1990), 171n4.

38. Russell and Kane, *The C Version*, 85, citing line 73's metrically unnecessary "oþer worse" and the non-alliterative line that follows, which are either a draft or "the reviser's note for development of the figure of counterfeit coin." This is part of their evidence that the C revision was uncompleted. For an opposing view, see Ralph Hanna, "A New Edition of the C Version," *YLS* 12 (1998): 184–85.

39. Justice, "Introduction," 5–8; Taylor, "Lost Revision," 129; Adams, "R/F MSS," 120–22.

40. While Adams mocks Kane and Donaldson for attributing to "pure coincidence" the absences of 15.511–28 and 533–69 from W-M and RF respectively ("R/F MSS," 120), he seems not to have any problem doing likewise with these cases (128, 126 respectively): there is nothing calling for mockery in either case. He invokes Ockham's razor against Kane and Donaldson's treatments of B 15.511–28 and 533–69 (120–21), but never mounts an argument against the attribution of 511–28's absence to eyeskip, which by Ockham's razor is manifestly the best interpretation. He instead falls back upon his arbitrary assumption that the two separate gaps must be connected: "This whole issue is clouded by KD's claim that a larger section of Bx here was misarranged" (127). The issue is not at all clouded: Kane and Donaldson's account is simple and straightforward.

41. Lines 17 from S, 18α–β from N², 23 from N, 27–28 from N², 31 from G, 35 from N², 38 from E, 49–57 from N², 54 from YPERMVA, 57 from D, 58 from G, 65 from N², 65α from PN², 79–80 from JG, 80 from N², 87 from SGN², 92–93 from N, 95 from N², 102b–104a from A, 107 from S, 109 from M, 126 from R, 131 from Y, 139 from DEA, 144 and 153 from N², 162 from R, 164–66 from P² (first two inserted by rubricator), 173–76 from A, 182 from G, 185b–86a and 194 from A, 213α from M, 235–35α from N², 241 from P², 264 from N, 265 and 269 from N², 275α from M, 279–80 from N², 287 from P² (inserted another hand), 293 from DQF, 306 from N², and 308–309 from VA.

42. Justice, "Introduction," 6, 7 (note that this Thomas is not the apostle and martyr as Justice has it, but the bishop, though the confusion is understandable: see Warner, "Becket," 115n22). Taylor, too, says that the "syntactical hash" of RF's text here "deviates from what one might expect to be produced by a native speaker of English, in the same manner as the utterance 'My dog has fleas and not to go fishing,'" which suggests to him that RF represents a later stage of text ("Lost Revision," 116).

43. RF/Cx readings to the left of the slash; W-M/Nx to the right: 529/279: And nat . . . to/That. 530/280: crepe in/crepe; confesse/and confessen. 531/281: amonges (R only)/ in (F/W-M/Nx as discussed below), Romaynes (F wild)/Romayne. 532/282: were/was.

44. See Warner, "Ur-B *Piers Plowman*," 33–36.

45. The derivation of RF's "no man" from C's "uch man" is straightforward enough, if wrong (and in any case, even if RF was copying Bx here, he turned "every" into "no" and omitted "for"); "shoneth" easily turned into "loveth" via confusion of "h" and "l" and minim trouble (see Kane, *The A Version*, 121); and "felachipp" and "companye," both absent from W-M, are synonyms.

46. See Warner, "Ur-B *Piers Plowman*," 23.

47. Kane and Donaldson, *The B Version*, 58–59, 168–69 and nn. Cf. Schmidt, *Parallel-Text*, 55–56.

48. Kane and Donaldson, *The B Version*, 67. I restore Bx's *courbed* (79), *And* (80), and *also* (81), since that and not Langland's text is what RF copied.

49. Ibid., 68. I restore R's *worse dede* (429) and W-M's *muche* (431).

50. 1) 10.297–308 initiates Langland's large-scale program of relocations at C 5.146–55. 2) 13.292–98 constitutes the first third of the third such relocation, to C 6.42–46 (just after 13.277–83 is transferred to C 6.30–37). 3) 13.436–53 ends three lines before the final one, of fifty-two lines (13.409–56 to C 7.69–116). 4) 13.399–408 bridges two long passages relocated to C 6 (13.358–98α and 13.409–56). In turning B into C, Langland would have marked the hundred-odd line passage for relocation, cancelling precisely these lines. 5) 11.160–70, from the Trajan episode, is replaced in C by a single new line (C 12.92).

## CHAPTER 4. THE ENDING, AND END, OF *PIERS PLOWMAN* B

1. Robert Worth Frank, Jr., *"Piers Plowman" and the Scheme of Salvation: An Interpretation of "Dowel, Dobet, and Dobest"* (New Haven, Conn.: Yale University Press, 1957), 118.

2. Skeat, *Vision of William*, 2:285, a sentiment often repeated.

3. For a critique of those datings of B that rely on either the attack on the papacy in 19.428–48 or the identity of Friar Flatterer in 20.313–15, see Stephen A. Barney, *The Penn Commentary on "Piers Plowman"*, vol. 5, *C Passus 20–22; B Passus 18–20* (Philadelphia: University of Pennsylvania Press, 2006), 174–76, 241.

4. Hanna, *London Literature*, 243. He argues, "B's conclusion and its revised opening can be viewed as precisely contemporary. The poem was finished, both in terms of its inner chronology and its imaginative structure, at a single moment," which he identifies as summer 1377 (250).

5. James Simpson, "'After Craftes Conseil clotheth yow and fede': Langland and London City Politics," in *England in the Fourteenth Century: Proceedings of the 1991 Harlaxton Symposium*, ed. Nicholas Rogers (Stamford, Conn.: P. Watkins, 1993), 109–27.

6. Grady, "Chaucer Reading Langland," 6 on the "incompleteness and irresolution" shared by both, and 20 on how "each poet resigns in what looks like frustration" and on "both poems' potential endlessness."

7. Justice, *Writing and Rebellion*, 129.

8. A number of manuscripts label these passus thus. See Robert Adams, "Reliability"

and "Langland's *Ordinatio*," whose argument that these rubrics are scribal my own findings support. See also discussion in the Preface.

9. Russell and Kane, *The C Version*, 82–83; Schmidt observes that "the extensive revision in 20, displaying Langland's art in unabated vigour, contrasts so strongly with the minimal changes in 21–22 as to lend prima facie support to R-K's understanding of the revision-process as terminated at 20 by the poet's illness or death" (*Parallel-Text*, 64; see also 161–62). Barney remarks, "A few lines that look very much like authorial revision rather than scribal variance challenge the Athlone conclusion," but does not comment upon the reasons for the lightness of whatever revision there might be (*Penn Commentary*, 100).

10. Russell and Kane remark that "these passus seem, to the modern eye, to contain some of the most powerful writing in the poem. But the same might be said of earlier passages which evidently no longer suited the plan of their poet" (*The C Version*, 82). Hanna proposes "a further possibility—that Langland did not consider revisions in this version as the utterly meticulous and thorough procedure which they imagine" ("New Edition," 179), but this does not seem any different from Russell and Kane's first possibility, that Langland was satisfied with this poetry; nor does it address the indications against that possibility.

11. Russell and Kane, *The C Version*, 82.

12. Ibid., 82–83. The Athlone editors do not mention what had earlier been for Russell the deciding factor against this possibility: the "slowing-down to the point of disappearance of the process of revision" in C 20. "Some Aspects of the Process of Revision in *Piers Plowman*," in *"Piers Plowman": Critical Approaches*, ed. S. S. Hussey (London: Methuen, 1969), 48; see also "Evolution," 44–45. Yet if the last two passus were not in B to begin with, then this slowing down is confined to the closing portions of passus 18, and appears much less dramatic. It would look like the work of someone eager to move on to his new, explosive conclusion to the poem: what is about to become passus 21–22 of his final revision. Russell's proposal might seem to court the objection put forth by Hanna, that "the editors must argue both sides of a single proposition—revision in the poem proceeded/did not proceed serially. The unrevised ending must strongly imply a serial procedure. On the other hand, the editors cannot opt for a serial theory because revision fails to show any uniform thoroughness throughout the poem, as it should do, had Langland gone through the work in order" ("New Edition," 179). Yet "random" means "random"; in these circumstances any portion of the poem, including the final two passus, could have been the final to be revised.

13. Russell and Kane, *The C Version*, 83.

14. Kane, *The A Version*, 38.

15. Morton W. Bloomfield, *"Piers Plowman" as a Fourteenth-Century Apocalypse* (New Brunswick, N.J.: Rutgers University Press, n.d. [1961]), 125. Barney remarks that here as at the opening of C 5 "the poem has just reached a kind of happy resolution" and, with reference to an earlier draft of this chapter, that if B ended with passus 18, "Such a conclusion may well have seemed appropriate" (*Penn Commentary*, 97–98).

16. Schmidt, *Parallel-Text*, 285. For Schmidt's "475–6" read "425–6" (= Kane-Donaldson B 18.423–24).

17. Robert Adams, "Glossing *Piers Plowman*: The New Penn Commentaries," *JEGP* 109 (2010): 77.

18. See Kane, "*Piers Plowman*: Problems and Methods of Editing the B-text," *Modern Language Review* 43 (1948): 8–18; Donaldson, *C-Text*, 232–47; Schmidt, *Parallel-Text*; and Adams, "Evidence." These early discussions by Kane and Donaldson rely in part on outmoded assumptions or partial evidence; indeed in the book's reprint Donaldson would disavow the premises upon which he bases this discussion (vi–vii).

19. These are discussed in Kane and Donaldson, *The B Version*, 116–21, 208–9, and Russell and Kane, *The C Version*, 129–36; a high proportion of these appear in the nineteen "lines with unmistakable defective alliteration" (ibid., 82n25).

20. On Bx's errors see Kane and Donaldson, *The B Version*, 90–95, and Russell and Kane, *The C Version*, 119–21, where they revisit about a dozen that Schmidt deems authorial; on Cx's, see Russell and Kane, 121–23 and nn40, 41. I say "clear" here because there are also about thirty slight differences between the two where it is nearly impossible to decide which is authorial; see Russell and Kane, 124–29.

21. It is indeed generally true that agreements in "major" errors are more reliable indicators of MS affiliations than are agreements in "minor" ones, which are often explicable as the results of coincident variation (see Schmidt, *Parallel-Text*, 40). Nevertheless to begin with such categorizations is to risk preempting the discovery of larger-scale patterns that cannot be thus explained, such as the $N^2$/W-M pattern of agreements (often in "minor" readings) over entire passages.

22. This sixty-three consists of all but one of Bx's errors (at 19.154 MS F, the sole representative of RF here, supports neither W-M nor Cx), and eleven of Cx's where RF or F(?=RF) supports the putative archetypal B reading: B 19/C 21 lines 42, 63, 373, 387; B 20/C 22 lines 83, 97, 128, 167 (R; F wild), 202, 282, 370. (In the remaining sixteen instances, RF or F(?=RF) either conflicts with W-M or is not extant: 19/21 lines 12, 109, 120, 142, 246, 267, 295, 339 (x2), 397, 435; 20/22 lines 1, 3, 7, 9, 38.) I do not consider readings from the category of slight differences between the two.

23. F alone, where R is lacking (i.e., all of B 19 and B 20.1–26), has agreements with C in passus 19/21, lines 12, 24, 39, 43, 46, 56–59, 64, 73, 77, 91, 94, 109, 118, 120, 130 (x2), 134, 140, 142, 145, 149, 151, 152, 154, 172α, 179, 181α, 183, 208, 223 (x2), 228, 236b–237a, 267, 274, 280, 283, 284, 295, 311, 330, 334, 336, 339 (x2), 343, 394, 446, 453, 463, 479, 479α, and passus 20/22, lines 1, 3, 7, 9, 11, 13. Both R and F agree with C in passus 20/22, lines 27, 37, 38 (x2), 39, 42, 55, 60, 62, 67, 78, 87, 93, 97, 102, 114, 119, 138, 139, 141, 183, 191, 194, 198, 208, 210, 211, 218, 221, 249, 253, 256, 260, 263, 277, 284, 291, 305, 310, 311, 320, 336, 342, 348, 350, 356, 382. The fact that the rate of RF/Cx readings upon the return of R continues, and even becomes denser, shows that F's agreements with Cx in passus 19/21 are those of RF (as Kane and Donaldson, *The B Version*, 165 and n86, and Schmidt, as below, believe as well).

24. Schmidt claims that in his edition the groups behave in an almost identical manner (*Parallel-Text*, 148). Kane and Donaldson judge W-M to err about 223 times through B 18 where R is extant (including those places where BmBoCot or O is not available), and thirty-three times in B 20 (*The B Version*, 54–57), and RF, 481 times through B 18, and

twenty-three times in B 20 (25–27). But the arbitrary nature of such statistics is indicated by the list of excluded categories, any of which on its own could potentially have a major impact. The exclusion of B 19 and 20.1–26 in these figures makes W-M look much more accurate than it is in either edition. Similarly, Kane and Donaldson's figures exclude readings where (1) any member of W-M does not contain the error attested by every other manuscript in that group, for whatever reason—say, B 20.356, where MS Bm alone, but not its siblings Bo or Cot, is deficient; (2) either R or F coincidentally agrees in error with W-M where the other, representing RF, has the correct reading (c. 130 instances; Kane and Donaldson, 58 and n90); (3) one W-M manuscript attests RF's error via coincident variation, as does MS L in thirteen variants (Kane and Donaldson, 58n89; Schmidt, 138–39); and (4) F, as it frequently does, errs even more wildly than R. On F's frequent wildness see Kane and Donaldson, 165–73; Schmidt, 143–44; and Robert Adams, Hoyt N. Duggan, Eric Eliason, Ralph Hanna, John Price-Wilkin, and Thorlac Turville-Petre, eds., *The Piers Plowman Electronic Archive*, vol. 1, *Corpus Christi College, Oxford MS 201 (F)* (Ann Arbor: University of Michigan Press, 2000).

25. Row 2, column 2 reads "unknowable" because of MS R's deficiency through B 20.26 and the wildness of F. Agreements of W-M/Cx against F would number in the hundreds (I find twelve in the first five lines of 19/21 alone), and only an unknown few of F's unique readings would attest the reading of RF, so that only the final 360 lines of passus B 20 provide valid comparison. The twenty-four RF/Cx agreements of column 1, row 1, occur in lines 12/10, 28/27 (x2), 85/87, 87/89, 101/104 (x2), 129/132, 147/150, 151/154, 157/160, 203/208, 262/270, 266/274, 270/278, 272/280, 275/297, 277/299, 296/329, 318/361, 359/398, 383/425, 401/444, 409/452. The rest of the agreements of column 1 are listed in note 23 above. The forty-three W-M/Cx agreements of column 2, row 1 occur in lines 41/40, 50/50, 59/59, 62/64, 69/71, 73/75, 76/78, 83/85, 84/86, 86/88, 93/96, 121/124, 124/127, 147/150, 158/161, 174/177, 180/183, 183/186, 190/195, 199/204, 205/210, 214/223, 219/228, 221/230, 234/243, 245/254, 246/255, 251/260, 252f./261f., 270/278, 277/299, 284/309, 291/321, 297/330, 299/332, 303/335 (x2), 321/364, 348/393, 353/396, 362/400, 390/432, 395/438. The nineteen W-M/Cx agreements of column 2, row 3 occur in lines 45, 65, 91, 132, 151, 152, 158, 166, 199, 202, 214, 233, 238f., 240 (x2), 265, 269, 289, 378.

26. On the basis of the figures of column 1, row 2 Hanna, "George Kane and the Invention of Textual Thought," argues that the exemplar used by R and F was deficient here, leading MS F to rely on a C exemplar for this passus. But indicators are unanimous that F's exemplar was from the B, not C family. It agrees with erroneous Bx in lines 97, 101, 148, 164, 174, 197, 243, 251, 253, 254, 271, 280, 292, 298, 301, 303, 308, 335, 343, 357, 362, 429, 437, 453, 477, and with correct Bx against erroneous Cx at lines 42, 63, 373 (a line not in the C tradition), and 387. Hanna notes that about fifteen of these erroneous Bx readings appear somewhere in the C record, but it is still much easier to grant what Hanna and everyone else has always believed, that F got these readings from its exemplar, rather than from consultation of various C manuscripts. (In any case this logic would have to apply to all B manuscripts, not just F, simply reducing the number of Bx errors in total, not F's percentage of Bx errors.) That RF came to agree so pervasively—indeed at almost the identical rate as does F here—with Cx in the following passus indicates that the F/

Cx agreements in 19/21 are part of a larger program to which R points as well upon its return. Hanna also tries to find evidence that F dips into C even after R's return, but the three or so instances he cites are of the most mundane sort in which that scribe frequently indulges (e.g., transposition, addition of initial *And*).

27. Over the previous nine passus, the density of W-M/Cx agreements vs. RF was about half again greater than that of RF/Cx agreements where we could be confident that RF was not contaminated by C (see the figures for those passus in Warner, "Ur-B *Piers Plowman*," 36–37), while here it is almost double. Perhaps the RF scribe got tired here and strayed from the correct reading more often than usual, but there might well be another explanation.

28. Barney, too, notes the importance of the density of RF/Cx agreements in "Do-best" in any attempt to edit, or even define, these two versions. He cites as two of the five major unresolved issues in the textual criticism of the poem the questions of whether Langland revised the last two passus and whether the RF and W-M families are in fact witnesses to an identical B text, to which the pattern of F/Cx agreements in B 19/C 21 pertains: "Are B and C mutually contaminated? . . . To what extent does agreement between RF and the C-Text reveal authorial readings? Are RF fully witnesses to the B-Text? Was the hypothetically corrupt C-Text archetype revised from a hypothetically corrupt B-Text manuscript with RF readings, or not? In short, given RF, just how distinct are the B-Text and the C-Text?" Barney, review of Schmidt's and Pearsall's first editions, *Speculum* 56 (1981): 165. These questions ostensibly refer to the status of RF in general, but the examples he cites are from B 19, and he remarks that these issues are intertwined (164).

29. The six rejected F/Cx readings, all in B 19, are lines 39, 134, and 339 (x2; his 342), where he chooses the W-M reading, and 12 and 295 (his 297), where he emends conjecturally. See his "Textual Notes" to these lines, *Parallel-Text*, 453–60.

30. Russell and Kane, *The C Version*, 122. It is unclear what import this "unassessable possibility" has in their explanation: if F and Cx could engage in coincidental agreement, then why not RF and Cx? This comment, and the fact that the editors identify so many fewer RF/Cx than F/Cx agreements in error, show that they recognize the force of my objection, and would not have felt comfortable assigning so many errors to RF and Cx in so few lines as they do to F and Cx.

31. I.e., with manuscripts S, G, H, Hm, and Cr; see Kane and Donaldson, *The B Version*, 28–32.

32. These appear in passus 19/21 lines 12, 24, 39, 46, 91, 109, 120, 134, 142, 151, 154, 183, 223 (x2), 228, 267, 280, 295, 311, 339 (x2), 479$\alpha$; passus 20/22, lines 1, 3, 7, 9, 11, 13. At one point, 19/21.140, Kane and Donaldson follow W-M, and Russell and Kane, RF/Cx. Russell and Kane, *The C Version*, 123 and n41, discuss eleven of these: seven where F alone agrees with all Cx, three where F=Cx but $N^2$ shares the correct reading with W-M, and one where the BmBoCot group of B shares the F/Cx reading. They treat two other instances, 19/21.154 and 311, without reference to F's reading, on 124, 125, where the choice could have gone either way, and remark that one, 20/22.1, was among the "few instances of straight choice" where they preferred the text of the B tradition (in this case, W-M), but without notice of F's agreement with Cx (121). Let me stress that my own solution

to these problems does not assume that every individual agreement of RF and Cx is the result of the pattern I identify. But if we begin to focus on the individual readings we might well overlook the overall pattern at issue.

33. MSS R and F share 504 errors (Kane and Donaldson, *The B Version*, 25–28); other major genetic groups include VH of A, 230 errors (Kane, *The A Version*, 72–73, 82–85); OC² of B, 330 errors through B 18 (Kane and Donaldson, 22–24); and VA of C, 443 (Russell and Kane, *The C Version*, 22–24).

34. I.e., six RF/Cx readings in B 18/C 20 where Russell and Kane prefer W-M (in lines 12/10, 129/132, 203/208, 272/280, 277/299, 409/452), and six from B 20/C 22 after R returns (in lines 38, 97, 139, 305, 311, 348). There are two other locations, 20/22.102 and 194, where Kane and Donaldson follow W-M and Russell and Kane follow RF/Cx, the second of which might suggest that the editors have taken on board Robert Adams's criticism ("Editing," 45n21) of their earlier attempt to find a meaningful distinction between the adverbs *wel* (W-M) and *ful* (RF/Cx).

35. And the final explanation to which those opposing my proposal might take recourse, that Cx consulted RF, falters on a point mentioned in the Preface: that RF's exemplar was itself contaminated by the tradition generated by Cx. That aside, such an idea would not explain why the Cx scribe turned to RF almost solely in the final two passus.

36. Donaldson remarks that "the poet himself thought of the passage as a movable insertion," a proposal Adams elaborates in arguing that these lines "probably filled one side of an inserted, attached leaf." Donaldson, "MSS R and F," 211; Adams, "R/F MSS," 121, as discussed in Chapter 3.

37. N² agrees with Cx at points of major divergence from Bx (lines 230, 239, 251–53, 369, 373). Even without reference to N²'s testimony, Barney cites one of these RF/Cx agreements, 20/22.37, as evidence that Langland revised these two passus: the line "explains the preceding two lines; it could be a late addition" (*Penn Commentary*, 202). He does not comment upon the process by which it would have been added to RF, but my proposal offers the only explanation that also accommodates N²'s tendency to agree with W-M at such points.

38. N²'s agreements with W-M occur in lines 12, 39, 43, 46 (approx.), 73, 94 (approx.), 120, 134, 149, 151, 181α, 223 (x2), 228, 274, 295, 336; it conflicts with both texts at lines 130 (x2), 154, 179, 267, 280, 283, 339, and 394; and for the remainder through line 425 (i.e., the lines in note 23 not cited here) it is a standard witness to Cx.

39. Russell and Kane, *The C Version*, 82n25.

40. Ibid., 83, with examples and discussion on 83–88. In a vein of critique similar to mine, Andrew Galloway writes, "The profiles of the zealous but hasty author and the zealous but clumsy literary executor acutely and non-idealistically define some of the real character of the C text; but by Occam's razor one may question why *two* figures are presented who seem hard to tell apart" ("Uncharacterizable Entities," 75), and Hanna comments upon the similarities between "the sloppy and meddlesome archetypal B scribe" and "the C executor incapable of bringing full order to Langland's foul papers" that the Athlone editors create ("New Edition," 183).

41. Schmidt, *Parallel-Text*, 285–86.

42. E. Talbot Donaldson voiced this point as well, with regard to the biased treatment of a new C line by opponents of Langland's authorship of that version: "It is impossible not to wonder, . . . if it had appeared in A and B and had been omitted by C, whether some one might not have complained that C was spoiling the picture" (*C-Text*, 74).

43. Barney, *Penn Commentary*, 101, with references to many studies elaborating the relationship.

44. Henry W. Wells, "The Construction of *Piers Plowman*," in *Interpretations of Piers Plowman*, ed. Edward Vasta (1929; Notre Dame, Ind.: University of Notre Dame Press, 1968), 6.

45. Anne Hudson finds some possible allusions to the revolt in the final two passus ("*Piers Plowman* and the Peasants' Revolt," 101, 102). In light of my findings her points might merit a new look.

## CONCLUSION: LOLLARS, FRIARS, AND *FYNDYNGES*: C PASSUS 9 AND THE CREATION OF *PIERS PLOWMAN*

1. In his commentary on this passage Stephen Barney directs readers to the friar's request that Meed fund a window in return for becoming "a suster of oure ordre" (C 3.54). Barney, *Penn Commentary*, 244.

2. Adams has recently argued that "such an upbeat reading of these final lines"—that is, that Conscience vows to become a pilgrim "*in order* that the friars might obtain an endowment, since they now are motivated to subvert Conscience by their fiscal insecurity and resultant flattery"—"would necessitate a massive re-glossing of many other derogatory phrases about the friars, lest students errantly make an otherwise logical inference: that Langland had no mixed feelings about them, despised them, and regarded them as unsalvageable toadies in the army of Antichrist"; Adams prefers R. E. Kaske's proposal that the sentence means "*And that the friars ever had a founding,* . . . may Nature now *avenge* me." Adams, "Glossing *Piers Plowman*," 80. But this ignores Anima's claim that "folke sholden *fynde*" anchorites, hermits, monks, *and friars*, who should not have to rely on the alms of tyrants, but should be able to live on the alms of upright and honest men (B 15.417–28α, discussed below), which is fully in keeping with the interpretation of the C version's concluding lines I here endorse.

3. Scase, "Two *Piers Plowman* C-Text Interpolations," 462, now supported by Kerby-Fulton, "Langland 'in His Working Clothes'?" Hanna's attempt to discredit Scase's argument does not seem to me successful (*Pursuing History*, 204–14); see especially the critiques by Galloway, "Uncharacterizable Entities," 71–74, and Kerby-Fulton, 140n3. Schmidt's refutation of Scase (*Parallel-Text*, 174–75) confines itself to analysis of the readings, and so ignores the evidence that leads her to posit the passages' existence on loose sheets in the first place.

4. Russell and Kane, *The C Version*, 102n23. The other new C passage that accords with these themes is of course the *apologia pro vita sua*, C 5.1–108, but there are no textual indications that it circulated independently. See the essays collected in Justice and

Kerby-Fulton, *Written Work*, especially Kathryn Kerby-Fulton, "Langland and the Bibliographic Ego," and Middleton, "Acts of Vagrancy."

5. Tar: Traugott Lawler, "Harlots' Holiness: The System of Absolution for Miswinning in the C Version of *Piers Plowman*," *YLS* 20 (2006): 186; *supersedeas*: John A. Alford, *"Piers Plowman": A Glossary of Legal Diction* (Cambridge: D.S. Brewer, 1988), s.v. I quote the Ilchester Prologue as presented in Kerby-Fulton, "Langland 'in His Working Clothes'," 162–67, following my usual policies (e.g., adding punctuation). This transcription's differences from Russell and Kane, Appendix II, *The C Version*, 186–94, are minor. Bracketed terms are damaged in the manuscript; some of these have left traces, supplied by Kerby-Fulton in brackets, but others are sourced from the received C 9 version.

6. Lawler, "Harlots' Holiness," 187.

7. Line 427, "Hir preyeres and hir penaunces to pees sholde brynge," recurs in C 17.236, "His preyeres with his pacience to pees sholde brynge," which itself appears amid the eighteen-line addition to the "poison of possession" lines. Lines 417, 419, and 420 combine to form C 17.35–36, "For wolde nevere faythfull god þat freres and monkes / Toke lyflode of luyther wynnynges in all here lyf tyme"; 424 reappears as C 17.48: "Thenne grace sholde growe ȝut and grene love wexe"; and 425 and 420 together constitute C 17.33–34, which says that beasts fed the hermits "In tokenynge þat trewe man alle tymes sholde / Fynde honest men and holy men and oþer rihtfole peple."

8. Donaldson, *C-Text*, 27, and Andrew Cole, *Literature and Heresy in the Age of Chaucer* (Cambridge: Cambridge University Press, 2008), 207n89, 217n92, connect the C passus 9 material with the opening lines of C passus 17.

9. Cole, *Literature and Heresy*, 44.

10. Ibid., 44–45. Cole, like Pearsall (*New Annotated Edition*, 181, n. to C 9.256–82) and others, understands these "wolves" to be the false hermits and "lollares." Lawler, by contrast, says: "If anything in this passage is to be connected with the false hermits, I would say it is the sheep (as in the opening lines of the poem). These hermits cannot be wolves: the harm they do is too limited. They are false friars but not false prophets"; in his mind the wolves "are clearly exploiters, whose donations are called 'raueners offrynges' at C 17.43 and 'rauenours Almesses' at C 17.47" ("Harlots' Holiness," 187). "Cannot" is perhaps an overstatement, especially if we recognize that these hermits are in league with Sir *Penetrans Domos* himself and thus do the greatest harm possible, but there is certainly room for Lawler's alternative reading, especially given the evidence of the Becket passus that some bishops themselves have turned into wolves in sheep's clothing (see Warner, "Becket"). A major reason for Holy Church Unity's downfall, after all, is Conscience's inability to recognize that Friar Flatterer/Sir *Penetrans Domos* is himself a wolf.

11. See Eggert, *Securing the Past*, 237–40.

12. John Norton-Smith, Introduction to *Bodleian Library MS Fairfax 16* (London: Scolar, 1979), vii–viii, ix. To support his argument that *Piers Plowman* A "was at best a coterie text and brought into circulation by the enthusiasm engendered by B and C," Hanna cites the analogy of "the circulation of Chaucer's canon, in which the later 'public poetry' precedes in circulation the earlier dream visions, with evidence for texts like *The Book of the Duchess* and *The House of Fame* remarkably belated." Hanna, *Pursuing History*,

199. Elsewhere, though, Hanna cites the *Book of the Duchess* as an example of how "early copies of texts often got read to pieces and thus do not survive for our scrutiny" (148), a phenomenon that elsewhere he seems to apply to *Piers Plowman* A (235), as discussed in Chapter 1. I am grateful to Andrew Cole for prompting me to consider the question of how my argument about the transmission of *Piers Plowman* compares with that of Chaucer's anthologized works.

# Bibliography

MANUSCRIPT AND EARLY PRINTED SOURCES

*Aberystwyth, National Library of Wales*
  MS 733B: *Piers Plowman* A/C splice, witnessing to the "ur-C" stage. http://www.
  llgc.org.uk/index.php?id=piersplowmannlwms733b.
*Bethlehem, Pennsylvania, Lehigh University*
  821.1 L265p 1550: Robert Crowley's first edition of *Piers Plowman* (STC 19906). Con-
  sulted online only: http://digital.lib.lehigh.edu/bookshelf, "Piers Plowman, 1505
  [1550]."
*Cambridge, Pembroke College*
  MS 312 C/6: fragment of A version of *Piers Plowman*.
*London, British Library*
  MS Cotton Vespasian B XVI: C version of *Piers Plowman*.
  MS Royal 7 E IV: John Bromyard's *Summa Praedicantium*.


PRINTED AND ELECTRONIC SOURCES

(primary sources listed by editor; *YLS* = *Yearbook of Langland Studies*)
Adams, Robert. "Editing *Piers Plowman B*: The Imperative of an Intermittently Critical
  Edition." *Studies in Bibliography* 45 (1992): 31–68.
———. "Evidence for the Stemma of the *Piers Plowman* B Manuscripts." *Studies in Bib-
  liography* 53 (2000): 173–94.
———. "Glossing *Piers Plowman*: The New Penn Commentaries." *JEGP* 109 (2010):
  71–81.
———. "The Kane-Donaldson Edition of *Piers Plowman*: Eclecticism's Ultima Thule."
  *Text* 16 (2006): 131–41.
———. "Langland's *Ordinatio*: The *Visio* and the *Vita* Once More." *YLS* 8 (1994): 51–
  84.
———. "The R/F MSS of *Piers Plowman* and the Pattern of Alpha/Beta Complementary
  Omissions: Implications for Critical Editing." *Text* 14 (2002): 109–37.
———. "The Reliability of the Rubrics in the B-Text of *Piers Plowman*." *Medium Ævum*
  54 (1985): 208–31.

————. Review of Russell and Kane, *Piers Plowman: The C Version*. *Speculum* 74 (1999): 1082–85.

Adams, Robert, Hoyt N. Duggan, Eric Eliason, Ralph Hanna, John Price-Wilkin, and Thorlac Turville-Petre, eds. *The Piers Plowman Electronic Archive*. Vol. 1, *Corpus Christi College, Oxford MS 201 (F)*. CD-ROM. Ann Arbor: University of Michigan Press, 2000.

Aers, David. Review of Justice and Kerby-Fulton, *Written Work*. *YLS* 12 (1998): 207–17.

Alford, John A. *"Piers Plowman": A Glossary of Legal Diction*. Cambridge: D.S. Brewer, 1988.

————. *"Piers Plowman": A Guide to the Quotations*. Binghamton, N.Y.: Medieval and Renaissance Texts and Studies, 1992.

————. "The Role of the Quotations in *Piers Plowman*." *Speculum* 52 (1977): 80–99.

Aston, Margaret. "Corpus Christi and Corpus Regni: Heresy and the Peasants' Revolt." *Past and Present* 143 (1994): 3–47.

Barney, Stephen A. *The Penn Commentary on "Piers Plowman"*. Vol. 5, *C Passus 20–22; B Passus 18–20*. Philadelphia: University of Pennsylvania Press, 2006.

————. Review of Pearsall and Schmidt 1978 editions. *Speculum* 56 (1981): 161–65.

————. "A Revised Edition of the C Text." *YLS* 23 (2009): 265–88.

Bennett, J. A. W. *Chaucer's "Book of Fame": An Exposition of "The House of Fame"*. Oxford: Clarendon, 1968.

Benskin, Michael. "The Letters <þ> and <y> in Later Middle English, and Some Related Matters." *Journal of the Society of Archivists* 7 (1982): 13–30.

Benson, C. David and Lynne Blanchfield. *The Manuscripts of "Piers Plowman": The B-Version*. Cambridge: D.S. Brewer, 1997.

Benson, Larry D., gen. ed. *The Riverside Chaucer*. Boston: Houghton Mifflin, 1987.

Bloomfield, Morton W. *"Piers Plowman" as a Fourteenth-Century Apocalypse*. New Brunswick, N.J.: Rutgers University Press, n.d. [1961].

*Bodleian MS Fairfax 16*. With an Introduction by John Norton-Smith. London: Scolar, 1979.

Bowers, Fredson. "Regularization and Normalization in Modern Critical Texts." *Studies in Bibliography* 42 (1989): 79–102.

Bowers, John M. *Chaucer and Langland: The Antagonistic Tradition*. Notre Dame, Ind.: University of Notre Dame Press, 2007.

————. *"Piers Plowman's* William Langland: Editing the Text, Writing the Author's Life." *YLS* 9 (1995): 65–90.

Brewer, Charlotte. *Editing "Piers Plowman": The Evolution of the Text*. Cambridge: Cambridge University Press, 1996.

Brundage, James A. *Law, Sex, and Christian Society in Medieval Europe*. Chicago: University of Chicago Press, 1987.

Bucci, Richard. "Tanselle's 'Editing without a Copy-Text': Genesis, Issues, Prospects." *Studies in Bibliography* 56 (2003–2004): 1–44.

Burrow, J. A. "The Structure of *Piers Plowman* B XV–XX: Evidence from the Rubrics." *Medium Ævum* 77 (2008): 306–12.

Carruthers, Mary. *The Search for St. Truth: A Study of Meaning in "Piers Plowman"*. Evanston, Ill.: Northwestern University Press, 1973.

Challoner, Richard, trans. *The Holy Bible*. Douay-Rheims translation. 1899. Baltimore: Tan Books, 1989.

Chambers, R. W. "The Manuscripts of *Piers Plowman* in the Huntington Library, and Their Value for Fixing the Text of the Poem." *Huntington Library Bulletin* 8 (1935): 1–25.

Chambers, R. W., and J. H. G. Grattan. "The Text of 'Piers Plowman'." *Modern Language Review* 26 (1931): 1–51.

Clopper, Lawrence M. "Langland's Markings for the Structure of *Piers Plowman*." *Modern Philology* 85 (1988): 245–55.

———. *"Songes of Rechelesnesse": Langland and the Franciscans*. Ann Arbor: University of Michigan Press, 1997.

Cole, Andrew. *Literature and Heresy in the Age of Chaucer*. Cambridge: Cambridge University Press, 2008.

Cooper, Helen. "The Four Last Things in Dante and Chaucer: Ugolino in the House of Rumour." *New Medieval Literatures* 3 (1999): 39–66.

———. "Langland's and Chaucer's Prologues." *YLS* 1 (1987): 71–81.

Cowen, Janet, and George Kane, eds. *Geoffrey Chaucer: "The Legend of Good Women"*. East Lansing, Mich.: Colleagues Press, 1995.

Dane, Joseph A. "Copy-Text and Its Variants in Some Recent Chaucer Editions." *Studies in Bibliography* 44 (1991): 164–83.

Davis, Bryan P. "The Rationale for a Copy of a Text: Constructing the Exemplar for British Library Additional MS. 10574." *YLS* 11 (1997): 141–55.

Davis, Isabel. *Writing Masculinity in the Later Middle Ages*. Cambridge: Cambridge University Press, 2007.

Donaldson, E. Talbot. "MSS R and F in the B-Tradition of *Piers Plowman*." *Transactions of the Connecticut Academy of Arts and Sciences* 39 (1955): 179–212.

———. *"Piers Plowman": The C-Text and Its Poet*. New Haven, Conn.: Yale University Press, 1949. Rpt. London: Frank Cass, 1966.

———. "The Psychology of Editors of Middle English Texts." In *Speaking of Chaucer*. New York: Norton, 1970. 102–18.

Doyle, A. I. "Remarks on Surviving Manuscripts of *Piers Plowman*." In *Medieval English Religious and Ethical Literature: Essays in Honour of G. H. Russell*, ed. Gregory Kratzmann and James Simpson. Cambridge: D.S. Brewer, 1986. 35–48.

Doyle, A. I., and M. B. Parkes. "The Production of Copies of the *Canterbury Tales* and the *Confessio Amantis* in the Early Fifteenth Century." In *Medieval Scribes, Manuscripts and Libraries: Essays Presented to N. R. Ker*, ed. M. B. Parkes and Andrew G. Watson. London: Scolar, 1978. 163–210.

Duggan, Hoyt N. "Creating an Electronic Archive of *Piers Plowman*." 1994. http://www.iath.virginia.edu/piers/report94.html (accessed February 28, 2009).

Economou, George D. "Chaucer and Langland: A Fellowship of Makers." In *Reading Medieval Culture: Essays in Honor of Robert W. Hanning*, ed. Robert M. Stein and

Sandra Pierson Prior. Notre Dame, Ind.: University of Notre Dame Press, 2005. 290–301.

Eggert, Paul. *Securing the Past: Conservation in Art, Architecture and Literature.* Cambridge: Cambridge University Press, 2009.

Fletcher, Alan J., Elaine M. Treharne, and Greg Walker. "Middle English: Excluding Chaucer." *Year's Work in English Studies* 77 (1996): 167–209.

Fowler, David C. "A New Edition of the B Text of *Piers Plowman.*" *Yearbook of English Studies* 7 (1977): 23–42.

———. "Star Gazing: Piers Plowman and the Peasants' Revolt." *Review* 18 (1996): 1–30.

Frank, Robert Worth, Jr. *"Piers Plowman" and the Scheme of Salvation: An Interpretation of "Dowel, Dobet, and Dobest".* New Haven, Conn.: Yale University Press, 1957.

Fyler, John M., ed. *The House of Fame.* In Benson, gen. ed., *The Riverside Chaucer.* 347–73, 977–90, 1139–43.

Galloway, Andrew. "Uncharacterizable Entities: The Poetics of Middle English Scribal Culture and the Definitive *Piers Plowman.*" *Studies in Bibliography* 52 (1999): 59–87.

Gradon, Pamela. "Langland and the Ideology of Dissent." *Proceedings of the British Academy* 66 (1980): 179–205.

Grady, Frank. "Chaucer Reading Langland: *The House of Fame.*" *Studies in the Age of Chaucer* 18 (1996): 3–23.

Green, Richard Firth. "John Ball's Letters: Literary History and Historical Literature." In *Chaucer's England: Literature in Historical Context,* ed. Barbara Hanawalt. Minneapolis: University of Minnesota Press, 1992. 176–200.

Greg, Walter W. "The Rationale of Copy-Text." In Greg, *Collected Papers,* ed. J. C. Maxwell. Oxford: Clarendon, 1966. 374–91.

Grindley, Carl. "The A-Version Ancestor of BmBoCot." *YLS* 24 (2010).

Gwynn, Aubrey. "The Date of the B-Text of *Piers Plowman.*" *Review of English Studies* 19 (1943): 1–24.

Hanna, Ralph. "Emendations to a 1993 'Vita de Ne'erdowel'." *YLS* 14 (2000): 185–98.

———. "George Kane and the Invention of Textual Thought: Retrospect and Prospect." *YLS* 24 (2010).

———. *London Literature, 1300–1380.* Cambridge: Cambridge University Press, 2005.

———. "A New Edition of the C Version." *YLS* 12 (1998): 175–88.

———. *Pursuing History: Middle English Manuscripts and Their Texts.* Stanford, Calif.: Stanford University Press, 1996.

———. "Studies in the Manuscripts of *Piers Plowman.*" *YLS* 7 (1993): 1–25.

———. *William Langland.* Aldershot: Variorum, 1993.

Hanna, Ralph, and Traugott Lawler, eds. *Boece.* In Benson, gen. ed., *The Riverside Chaucer.* 395–469, 1003–19, 1151–60.

Hervieux, Léopold, ed. *Les Fabulistes Latins: Dupuis le siècle d'Auguste jusq' à la fin du moyen âge.* Vol. 4, *eudes de Cheriton et ses dérivés.* 1896. New York: Olms, 1970.

Hiatt, Alfred. *The Making of Medieval Forgeries: False Documents in Fifteenth-Century England.* Toronto: University of Toronto Press, 2004.

Horobin, Simon. "Harley 3954 and the Audience of *Piers Plowman*." In *Medieval Texts in Context*, ed. Graham D. Caie and Denis Renevey. New York: Routledge, 2008. 68–84.

———. " 'In London and Opelond': The Dialect and Circulation of the C Version of *Piers Plowman*." *Medium Ævum* 74 (2005): 248–69.

Horobin, Simon, and Linne R. Mooney. "A *Piers Plowman* Manuscript by the Hengwrt/Ellesmere Scribe and Its Implications for London Standard English." *Studies in the Age of Chaucer* 26 (2004): 65–112.

Hudson, Anne. "Langland and Lollardy?" *YLS* 17 (2003): 93–105.

———. "*Piers Plowman* and the Peasants' Revolt: A Problem Revisited." *YLS* 8 (1994): 85–106.

———. *The Premature Reformation: Wycliffite Texts and Lollard History*. Oxford: Clarendon, 1988.

Justice, Steven. "Introduction: Authorial Work and Literary Ideology." In Justice and Kerby-Fulton, *Written Work*. 1–12.

———. *Writing and Rebellion: England in 1381*. Berkeley: University of California Press, 1994.

Justice, Steven, and Kathryn Kerby-Fulton, eds. *Written Work: Langland, Labor, and Authorship*. Philadelphia: University of Pennsylvania Press, 1997.

Kane, George. "Langland: Labour and 'Authorship'." *Notes and Queries* n.s. 45 (1998): 420–25.

———. "Langland, William (c.1325–c.1390)." In *Oxford Dictionary of National Biography*, ed. H. C. G. Matthew and Brian Harrison. Oxford: Oxford University Press, 2004. http://www.oxforddnb.com/view/article/16021 (accessed November 4, 2008).

———, ed. *"Piers Plowman": The A Version*. Rev. ed. Berkeley: University of California Press, 1988.

———. *"Piers Plowman": Glossary*. New York: Continuum, 2005.

———. *"Piers Plowman*: Problems and Methods of Editing the B-Text." *Modern Language Review* 43 (1948): 1–25.

———. "The 'Z Version' of *Piers Plowman*." *Speculum* 60 (1985): 910–30.

Kane, George, and E. Talbot Donaldson, eds. *"Piers Plowman": The B Version*. Rev. ed. Berkeley: University of California Press, 1988.

Kelly, Henry Ansgar. "Uniformity and Sense in Editing and Citing Medieval Texts." *Medieval Academy News* 148 (Spring 2004): 8–9.

Kerby-Fulton, Kathryn. *Books Under Suspicion: Censorship and Tolerance of Revelatory Writing in Late Medieval England*. Notre Dame, Ind.: University of Notre Dame Press, 2006.

———. "Langland and the Bibliographic Ego." In Justice and Kerby-Fulton, *Written Work*. 67–143.

———. "Langland 'in His Working Clothes'? Scribe D, Authorial Loose Revision Material, and the Nature of Scribal Intervention." In *Middle English Poetry: Texts and Traditions: Essays in Honour of Derek Pearsall*, ed. A. J. Minnis. York: York Medieval Press, 2001. 139–67.

————. Review of *YLS* 8 (1994). *Modern Language Review* 93 (1998): 458–59.

Kerby-Fulton, Kathryn, and Steven Justice. "Scribe D and the Marketing of Ricardian Literature." In *The Medieval Professional Reader at Work: Evidence from Manuscripts of Chaucer, Langland, Kempe, and Gower*, ed. Kathryn Kerby-Fulton and Maidie Hilmo. Victoria, B.C.: University of Victoria, 2001. 217–37.

Kirk, Elizabeth D. "Langland's Plowman and the Recreation of Fourteenth-Century Religious Metaphor." *YLS* 2 (1988): 1–21.

Kirk, Elizabeth D., and Judith H. Anderson, eds. *"Piers Plowman": An Alliterative Verse Translation by E. Talbot Donaldson*. New York: Norton, 1990.

Lawler, Traugott. "Harlots' Holiness: The System of Absolution for Miswinning in the C Version of *Piers Plowman*." *YLS* 20 (2006): 141–89.

Lyman, Gene. "Scribal Grapholects: Allographic Substitutions and the Textual Transmission of *Piers Plowman* B." Presented at the Fourth International *Piers Plowman* Conference, University of Pennsylvania, May 17, 2007.

Lynch, Kathryn L. "Dating Chaucer." *Chaucer Review* 42 (2007): 1–22.

Machan, Tim William. *Textual Criticism and Middle English Texts*. Charlottesville: University Press of Virginia, 1994.

Mann, Jill. "The Power of the Alphabet: A Reassessment of the Relation between the A and the B Versions of *Piers Plowman*." *YLS* 8 (1994): 21–50.

McGann, Jerome. *Radiant Textuality: Literature After the World Wide Web*. New York: Palgrave Macmillan, 2001.

McIntosh, Angus, M. L. Samuels, and Michael Benskin, eds. *A Linguistic Atlas of Late Mediaeval English*. 4 vols. Aberdeen: Aberdeen University Press, 1986.

Meroney, Howard. "The Life and Death of Longe Wille." *ELH* 17 (1950): 1–35.

*Middle English Dictionary*. Ed. Hans Kurath et al. Ann Arbor: University of Michigan Press, 1952–2001. http://quod.lib.umich.edu/m/med/.

Middleton, Anne. "Acts of Vagrancy: The C Version 'Autobiography' and the Statute of 1388." In Justice and Kerby-Fulton, *Written Work*. 208–317.

Mooney, Linne R. "Chaucer's Scribe." *Speculum* 81 (2006): 97–138.

Patterson, Lee. *Negotiating the Past: The Historical Understanding of Medieval Literature*. Madison: University of Wisconsin Press, 1987.

Pearsall, Derek. "The 'Ilchester' Manuscript of *Piers Plowman*." *Neuphilologische Mitteilungen* 82 (1981): 181–93.

————. *The Life of Geoffrey Chaucer: A Critical Biography*. Oxford: Blackwell, 1992.

————, ed. *"Piers Plowman": A New Annotated Edition of the C-text*. Exeter: University of Exeter Press, 2008.

————. Review of Kane and Donaldson, *The B Version*. *Medium Ævum* 46 (1977): 278–85.

Rigg, A. G., and Charlotte Brewer, eds. *"Piers Plowman": The Z Version*. Toronto: Pontifical Institute of Mediaeval Studies, 1983.

Russell, George H. "The Evolution of a Poem: Some Reflections on the Textual Tradition of *Piers Plowman*." *Arts: The Proceedings of the Sydney University Arts Association* 2 (1962): 33–46.

———. "Some Aspects of the Process of Revision in *Piers Plowman*." In *"Piers Plowman": Critical Approaches*, ed. S. S. Hussey. London: Methuen, 1969. 27–49.

Russell, George H., and George Kane, eds. *"Piers Plowman": The C Version*. Berkeley: University of California Press, 1997.

Russell, George H., and Venetia Nathan. "A *Piers Plowman* Manuscript in the Huntington Library." *Huntington Library Quarterly* 26 (1963): 119–30.

Samuels, M. L. "Langland's Dialect." *Medium Ævum* 54 (1985): 232–47.

Sargent, Michael G. "What Do the Numbers Mean? A Textual Critic's Observations on Some Patterns of Middle English Manuscript Transmission." In *Design and Distribution of Late Medieval Manuscripts in England*, ed. Margaret Connolly and Linne R. Mooney. York: York Medieval Press, 2008. 205–44.

Scase, Wendy. *"Piers Plowman" and the New Anticlericalism*. Cambridge: Cambridge University Press, 1989.

———. "Two *Piers Plowman* C-Text Interpolations: Evidence for a Second Textual Tradition." *Notes and Queries* n.s. 34 (1987): 456–63.

Schmidt, A. V. C. *"Piers Plowman": A Parallel-Text Edition of the A, B, C and Z Versions*. Vol. 2, *Introduction, Textual Notes, Commentary, Bibliography and Indexical Glossary*. Kalamazoo, Mich.: Medieval Institute Publications, 2008.

Simpson, James. "'After Craftes Conseil clotheth yow and fede': Langland and London City Politics." In *England in the Fourteenth Century: Proceedings of the 1991 Harlaxton Symposium*, ed. Nicholas Rogers. Stamford, Conn.: P. Watkins, 1993. 109–27.

Skeat, Walter W., ed. *The Vision of William Concerning Piers the Plowman: In Three Parallel Texts*. 2 vols. 1886. Oxford: Oxford University Press, 1969.

Somerset, Fiona. *Clerical Discourse and Lay Audience in Late Medieval England*. Cambridge: Cambridge University Press, 1998.

Steiner, Emily. "Radical Historiography: Langland, Trevisa, and the *Polychronicon*." *Studies in the Age of Chaucer* 27 (2005): 171–211.

Tanselle, G. Thomas. "Editing without a Copy-Text." *Studies in Bibliography* 47 (1994): 1–22.

Tavormina, M. Teresa. "*Piers Plowman* and the Liturgy of St. Lawrence: Composition and Revision in Langland's Poetry." *Studies in Philology* 84 (1987): 245–71.

Taylor, Sean. "The Lost Revision of *Piers Plowman B*." *YLS* 11 (1997): 97–134.

Thorne, John. "Updating *Piers Plowman* Passus 3: An Editorial Agenda in Huntington Library MS Hm 114." *YLS* 20 (2006): 67–92.

Thorne, J. R., and Marie-Claire Uhart. "Robert Crowley's *Piers Plowman*." *Medium Ævum* 55 (1986): 248–54.

Turville-Petre, Thorlac. "Sir Adrian Fortescue and his Copy of *Piers Plowman*." *YLS* 14 (2000): 29–48.

Warner, Lawrence. "Becket and the Hopping Bishops." *YLS* 17 (2003): 107–34.

———. "The Gentleman's *Piers Plowman*: John Mitford and his Annotated Copy of the 1550 Edition of William Langland's Great Poem." *La Trobe Journal* 84 (2009): 104–12, 130–31.

————. "The Ur-B *Piers Plowman* and the Earliest Production of C and B." *YLS* 16 (2002): 3–39.

Weber, Robert, ed. *Biblia Sacra: Iuxta Vulgatam Versionem.* 3rd ed. Stuttgart: Deutsche Bibelgesellschaft, 1983.

Wells, Henry W. "The Construction of *Piers Plowman.*" 1929. Rpt. in *Interpretations of "Piers Plowman"*, ed. Edward Vasta. Notre Dame, Ind.: University of Notre Dame Press, 1968. 1–21.

Windeatt, Barry, ed. *English Mystics of the Middle Ages.* Cambridge: Cambridge University Press, 1994.

Wittig, Joseph S. *"Piers Plowman": Concordance.* London: Athlone, 2001.

Wrenn, C. L. Review of Kane, *The A Version. Modern Language Notes* 76 (1961): 856–63.

Wright, Thomas. *Thomas Wright's Political Songs of England: From the Reign of John to that of Edward II.* Ed. Peter Cross. 1939. Cambridge: Cambridge University Press, 1996.

# Index

*Acknowledgments*

In September 2001, out for a pleasant stroll with George Russell along the banks of Canberra's Lake Burley-Griffin, I wondered what on earth I could ask this great scholar that would not reveal too much of my ignorance about his edition. My own background was far removed from his, but I was fresh from a draft of an essay on the Becket lines of B 15/C 17, and so had a back-up plan. I asked him why, at C 17.279, a single C manuscript ($N^2$) agreed with the rejected W-M reading of B. The reply surprised me: "Really? These things have a tendency to be much bigger than they at first appear. I'll have to think about that." My gratitude for George's support and advice during my initiation into the world of *Piers Plowman* textual studies is deep and lasting; I only wish he had lived to see the fruits of that first conversation. On a separate note, I would also like to acknowledge the debt that this book owes to all editors of the poem, especially George Russell and his colleagues, George Kane and E. Talbot Donaldson.

The initial ideas upon which this book elaborates were first published in the 2002 volume of *The Yearbook of Langland Studies*, a journal that from 2004 I have co-edited with Andrew Cole and Fiona Somerset. It has been a pleasure to work with Patricia Hollahan and the staff of Medieval Institute Publications, and now with Simon Forde and the staff of Brepols. My fortune in having Andrew and Fiona as daily e-mail correspondents knows no limits; thanks especially to Andrew for his feedback on a number of concrete matters in this book. Andrew Galloway, initially in his capacity as previous editor of *YLS*, has been a generous mentor. At the 2007 Philadelphia *Piers Plowman* conference I polled the audience on their favorite: Buddy, Elvis, or Andy? Andy won easily. He had probably advised all of them as much as he did me on much of the material in this book.

I am grateful to my colleagues from my time at Penn in the 1990s, who, across the world though I now am, have remained friends: David Lorenzo Boyd, Kevin Brownlee, Rita Copeland, Ann Matter, Jim O'Donnell, Emily Steiner, Siegfried Wenzel, and especially David Wallace. The three readers for Penn Press, of whom Stephen Barney and Derek Pearsall identified themselves, provided trenchant and detailed recommendations for revision, which have helped me to improve this book immeasurably. I presented the findings of Chapter 4 on a panel on the occasion of the publication of Derek's revised C edition at the Medieval Academy of America meeting in Vancouver, 2008; thanks to Kathryn Kerby-Fulton for the invitation and lively discussion.

Since 2004 Carl Schmidt and I have engaged in an enjoyable conversation, full of spirited disagreement (and even occasional agreement) about textual matters, on email and in person where possible. I am especially grateful for his valuable guidance on an earlier stage of Chapter 4. In the medievalist community Simon Horobin, Linne Mooney, and Wendy Scase have been especially generous with their time and expertise. I presented much of this material at workshops held by the Piers Plowman Electronic Archive in Charlottesville, 2004 and 2005, sponsored by the British Academy and the University of Virginia, and am grateful especially to its guiding spirit Dug Duggan, as well as to Robert Adams, Patricia Bart, Carter Hailey, Stephen Shepherd, Thorlac Turville-Petre, and Michael Calabrese. My colleagues in Australia have provided a rich, vibrant, and, yes, fun intellectual community. Thanks in particular to Dan Anlezark, Geraldine Barnes, Tom Burton, Margaret Clunies Ross, Louise D'Arcens, Paul Eggert, Janet Hadley Williams, Heather Kerr, Andrew Lynch, Jenna Mead, Roger Osborne, Nicola Parsons, Lucy Potter, Margaret Rogerson, Anne Scott, Stephanie Trigg, and Andrea Williams.

The Australian Academy of the Humanities supported my visit to the National Library of Wales in 2003, where Ceridwen Lloyd-Morgan shared her vast knowledge of MS 733B and facilitated my work with, and the subsequent digitization of, that manuscript. The Faculty of Humanities and Social Sciences of the University of Adelaide contributed to the costs of that digitization and supported my participation in the *PPEA* workshops. The Faculty of Arts of the University of Sydney enabled me to engage the services of Stephanie Downes as proof-reader and indexer. And Jerry Singerman of Penn Press has responded with alacrity, not to mention fairness and refreshing wit, to my inquiries and missives, from initial proposal to delivery of the final manuscript. If medieval studies is in great shape—and I certainly think it is—it is in no small part thanks to Jerry's efforts. Thanks too to Caroline Winschel and especially Alison Anderson at Penn Press for producing this handsome book.

Chapter 4 is a revision of "The Ending, and End, of *Piers Plowman* B: The C-Version Origins of the Final Two Passus," *Medium Ævum* 76 (2007): 225–50, © 2007 Society for the Study of Medieval Languages and Literature.

One paragraph of the Conclusion appeared in *"Piers Plowman* B XV 417–28a: An Intrusion from Langland's C Papers?" *Notes & Queries* 51, 2 (2004): 119–22, published by Oxford University Press.

Finally, and most happily, let me express my love for my family, especially my parents, Seth and Emily Warner, and my parents-in-law, Kevin and Jan Marjoribanks. Emily and Kevin would have liked nothing more than to see this book in print: and I have no doubt they would have its best readers. My son Sebastian has been an utter delight, so much so that the day he asked "is that Middle English?" followed immediately by "do you want to be Darth Vader?" when I was reading the sports pages over breakfast wasn't even the highlight of his fifth year. Most of all, I thank my wife, Genevieve Marjoribanks, for her love, support, sense of style, and *joie de vivre*, whether the playground is London, Philadelphia, Canberra, Adelaide, or Sydney. Or beyond. This book is for Genevieve with all my love.